PuT 01/13
DS 05/16

CRYSTAL CLEAR
CRYSTAL CLEAR
CRYSTAL CLEAR

641'
598
I
SCFW

P

AN

This book should be returned/renewed by the
latest date shown above. Overdue items incur
charges which prevent self-service renewals.
Please contact the library.

Wandsworth Libraries
24 hour Renewal Hotline
01159 293388
www.wandsworth.gov.uk

THE BRIGHTER B
Wand

D1422177

9030 00003 0243 7

COOK BRAZILIAN

100 CLASSIC AND CREATIVE RECIPES

Leticia Moreinos Schwartz

PHOTOGRAPHY BY BEN FINK

KYLE CATHIE LIMITED

This paperback edition published in Great Britain in 2012
by Kyle Books
an imprint of Kyle Cathie Ltd
23 Howland Street, London W1T 4AY
www.kylebooks.com

First published in hardback in Great Britain in 2010

All rights reserved. No reproduction, copy or transmission of this
publication may be made without written permission. No paragraph
of this publication may be reproduced, copied or transmitted save
with the written permission or in accordance with the provision
of the Copyright Act 1956 (as amended). Any person who does any
unauthorised act in relation to this publication may be liable
to criminal prosecution and civil claims for damages.

Text © 2010 Leticia Schwartz
Finished food photography © 2010 Ben Fink
Location photography © 2010 Luciano Bogado
Book design © 2010 Kyle Cathie Limited

Project editor Anja Schmidt
Designer Jee Chang, Black Paper Design
Food styling Susan Vajaranant
Prop styling Roy Finamore
Copyeditor Ann Cahn
Production Lisa Pinnell and Gemma John

ISBN 978-0-85783-154-5

A cataloging-in-publication record for this title is available from
the British Library.

Colour reproduction by Sang Choy
Printed and bound in C&C OFFSET Printing CO.,LTD

LONDON BOROUGH OF WANDSWORTH	
9030 00003 0243 7	
Askews & Holts	10-Jan-2013
641.5981	£15.99
	WWX0010314/0180

TABLE OF CONTENTS

A MISSION OF JOY AND LOVE

Think of Brazil and you think of football, samba, bossa-nova, beaches and carnival. Behind these popular assets lies an incredibly rich cuisine that is present in every aspect of Brazilian culture. Most cookery books group Brazil in the same pot as Latin American cuisine since they share many ingredients. But our history differs in many ways and it impacts on the application, taste and approach of our cooking. To understand Brazilian cooking, you have to understand Brazil: unlike the rest of South America, which was colonised by Spain, Brazil was colonised by Portugal. Our cuisine is represented by three different cultures: the Portuguese, the Africans (who were brought to Brazil for agricultural labour) and the native Indians. This three-way mixture is the essence of our culture: it's in the music we hear, in the foods that we eat and in the faces of our people.

The Portuguese brought their love for salt cod, *linguiça*, soups, stews and lots of sweets, mostly based on egg yolks and sugar. The Africans brought their love for palm oil, peanuts and cashews, rice and beans, and *carne seca*. The native Indians brought their love for yucca, coconut, fish, spices and exotic fruits. Blend the three, add some centuries, and the result is a magnificent combination of delicious and exotic dishes prepared with techniques, ingredients and elements from all three cultures that meet in the same pan. I particularly love the fragrance of *dendê* – the smell of Africa in a bottle of oil, the sweetness of coconut milk bubbling in a *moqueca*, the sound of a pressure cooker full of beans and the remarkable connection to Brazil I feel every time I make these dishes.

This book is a celebration of this fantastic cuisine and of Brazilian culture. I was born and raised in Ipanema, where life was good with the beach, cosmopolitan culture, parties, music – and lots of food. Some cooks thank their mothers and grandmothers for their love of cooking. I thank our housekeeper, an incredible cook who, like many other Brazilians, didn't rely on any written recipe. By the age of eight, I was hypnotised by the power of her cooking and my parents bought me my first recipe notebook. I began writing in it with the first things I ever cooked – *Pão de Queijo*,

fluffy little cheese breads (see page 16) and *Brigadeiros*, chocolate fudge balls (see page 132). Cooking the dishes I grew up eating is the way I found to reconnect with my country after I left it to study at The French Culinary Institute in New York City. There are a few demanding recipes, I'll confess, such as the Empadão de Frango on page 92, and to make it easier I like to prepare the dough and filling one day in advance and assemble them on the next day. But what strikes me about Brazilian cuisine is that there is always a casual feel and an elegant simplicity to our cooking that derives from our culture.

The recipes in *Cook Brazilian* include classic dishes with some inspirational recipes thrown in. My goal with this book is to teach you something you don't know about Brazilian cuisine, and to inspire you to cook dishes you haven't considered before, incorporating this cuisine into your home kitchen just as you might with Italian, French or Indian.

In addition to some of my favourites, I also tweaked some recipes to my taste. When I lived in Brazil, I loved many of these dishes the way they are traditionally made. But after 12 years of working as a chef in America, my palate has changed. Now I find some stews too heavy, a few of the *petiscos* (bar foods) too big, and many of the sweets too sweet.

There are a few demanding recipes, I'll confess, such as the *Empadão de Frango* on page 92, and to make it easier I like to prepare the dough and filling in advance and assemble the next day. But what strikes me about Brazilian cuisine is that there is always a casual feel and an elegant simplicity to our cooking that derives from our culture.

Brazil's food world today

The culture behind Brazilian gastronomy and food writing is very young. It's been only a decade or so since we started celebrating the profession of chef in Brazil and cherishing our native ingredients. Until then, yucca, *dendê* oil, coconut and beans were seen as peasant food.

Brazil has been adopted by many international chefs, who went to Brazil to live and work, fell in love with the country and never left. One of the most esteemed is Claude Troisgros, son of legendary chef Pierre Troisgros, owner of the restaurant Troisgros, in Roanne, France. After 27 years in Rio, Claude is now a *carioca* at heart, exploring exotic Brazilian ingredients combined with French technique to create amazing dishes. In São Paulo culinary practitioners such as Emanuel Bassoleil and Laurant Sadeau are among others who have chosen Brazil as their new home, and realised what a huge resource its local ingredients offer.

For many years Rio de Janeiro and São Paulo were considered the two metropolitan areas that dominated tourism. This is no longer the case as other cities are fast becoming food destinations, too, including Tiradentes in Minas Gerais, which now has restaurants such as Tulha Du Chef as well as gastronomic festivals. In Belém-do-Para, the capital of the state of Pará, chef Paulo Martins in his restaurant, Lá em Casa, is exploring the heart of the Amazon, using ingredients most of us have never even seen or heard of. In Bahia, the restaurant Tempero da Dada has attracted tourists from around the world.

It's so exciting to see the culinary landscape change. Brazilian-born chefs are now also working with Brazilian ingredients, such as Ludmilla Soeiro and Roberta Sudbrack in Rio, the above-mentioned Paulo Martins in Belemdo-Para, Carla Pernambuco, Ana Luiza Trajano and Alex Atala in São Paulo, to name just a few. These chefs are creating amazing dishes such as Guava Paste Soufflé with Mascarpone Sauce (page 144), Yucca Sticks (page 34) and Baked Coconut (page 168). I am delighted to feature such contemporary recipes in this book. Now, when you think about Brazil, you won't just think of football and carnival. Trust me on this: you'll think food.

Bar Food
Petiscos

CAIPIRINHA

Refreshing, cool, sweet and festive, *caipirinha* is Brazil. And if *caipirinha* is Brazil, then *cachaça* (see Glossary on page 170) is our national shrine. *Caipirinha* is a simple cocktail based on a mixture of mashed lime with sugar, ice and *cachaça*. There are a few variables, however, that make all the difference. The lime should be cut into medium chunks, then mashed with sugar by a wooden muddler until the lime releases its oil. Transfer to a shaker, add some ice and *cachaça*, shake and pour. Some recipes advise against mashing the lime too hard, as the oil can taste bitter. That's a very legitimate argument, but the sugar protects it and the more you release those oils, the better. Remember that *caipirinha* calls for lime and not lemon. Lemon skin is much thicker and carries a heavier white layer, giving a stronger, bitter taste. I like my *caipirinha* on the lighter side, although it's very common to use a stronger dose than suggested here. *Caipirinha* is not the type of drink to serve out of a pitcher or prepare in advance. Each must be prepared individually, shaken individually and immediately poured into a wide, sturdy glass.

MAKES 1 CAIPIRINHA

2 limes
1 tablespoon sugar
2–3 tablespoons cachaça (adjust amount to taste)
ice cubes

1   Trim the ends off the limes. Cut the limes into medium-sized wedges.

2   Using a muddler, or the end of a wooden spoon, mash the lime with the sugar, making sure to squeeze all the juices from the lime and to dissolve the sugar in the juice.

3   Transfer the lime mixture to a shaker. Add the *cachaça* and ice cubes. Shake well (about 8–10 times) and pour into a large but not tall, sturdy glass.

PLAYING WITH CACHAÇA

Use other citrus fruit to make *caipirinhas*, but keep in mind the white layer mentioned above; as long as you use a citrus with a thin skin – and that may vary from citrus to citrus – your *caipirinha* will taste great. Berries make a sweet and colourful drink as well. Strawberries? Call it Caipi-rubi. Vodka? Caipiroska. The ingredients below are also delicious.

Proceed as the caipirinha recipe on the left, substituting the orange for the lime. Add the mint leaves to the shaker with the orange-sugar mixture.

MAKES 1 CAIPIRINHA

1 orange
1 teaspoon sugar
2 tablespoons cachaçca
4–5 mint leaves

CHEESE BREAD

Pão de Queijo

A soft, chewy bread roll about the size of a golf ball infused with cheesy flavour, *pão de queijo* is Brazil's favourite savoury snack and an excellent recipe to add to your repertoire. The manioc starch (see Glossary on page 170) is what gives the cheese roll an incredible gooey and chewy texture, so try your best to use both types of manioc starches. I always buy manioc starch in big quantities so that whenever I decide to make *pao de queijo*, and that is quite often,

I don't have to go hunting for it. A few online sources are www.ipanemagirl.net, www.amigofoods.com and www.sendexnet. com. You can prepare the recipe ahead of time and freeze the little rolls unbaked for up to 3 months. Just pop one in the oven directly from the freezer and in 12–15 minutes you'll have deliciously cheesy treats!

225g (8 oz) finely grated fresh Parmesan
   (or Pecorino Romano)
2 large eggs
2 egg yolks
225g (8 oz) sour manioc starch (*povilho azedo*)
130g (4½ oz) sweet manioc starch (*povilho doce*)
2 teaspoons sea salt
125ml (4fl oz) full-fat milk
125ml (4fl oz) water
90ml (3fl oz) extra virgin olive oil
pinch of ground nutmeg
pinch of cayenne pepper
pinch of black pepper

1   Place the grated Parmesan in the bowl of a food processor. Add the whole eggs and yolks and blend until you have a smooth paste, about 1 minute. Set aside.

2   Place the 2 starches and salt in the bowl of an electric mixer fitted with the paddle attachment. Set aside.

3   Place the milk, water and olive oil in a small saucepan and bring to the boil. Immediately pour the milk mixture all at once into the starch mixture and turn the machine on at low speed. Mix until the dough is smooth and the starch is all incorporated, about 2 minutes.

4   Pause the machine and add the cheese and egg paste, scraping directly into the manioc starch mixture. Add the nutmeg, cayenne and black pepper. Mix the dough at low speed until it turns a pale yellow, about 10 minutes. You are trying to develop the structure of the dough by kneading it slowly. The dough is moist and sticky.

5   Transfer the dough to a bowl, cover it with clingfilm, and chill for at least 2 hours in the refrigerator, or overnight.

6   Preheat the oven to 180°C/350°F/Gas Mark 4. Line a baking sheet with baking paper.

7   Wet your hands with olive oil (alternatively, you can flour your hands with manioc starch) and use an ice-cream scoop as portion control to make 2.5-cm (1-inch) balls, rolling them with your hands. Place them on the baking sheet, leaving about 4–5 cm (1½–2 inches) between each roll (or you can freeze them at this point by storing them in a zip-lock plastic bag for up to 3 months).

8   Bake the cheese rolls in the oven until they puff up and look lightly golden brown, about 12–14 minutes. To ensure even baking, rotate the sheet once during baking time.

9   Remove the baking sheet from the oven and place the rolls in a basket lined with a napkin. Serve immediately while they are still at their warmest and chewiest.

COD FRITTERS

Bolinhos de Bacalhau

This is the granddaddy of bar foods served in *boutequins* all over Brazil. An exquisite deep-fried morsel that usually comes in a basket, cod fritters come in many variations. What makes this particular recipe so delicious and different are the egg whites mixed into the batter, which provide the fritters with a delicate, airy texture. When buying salt cod, try to find a piece that looks very meaty. Allow a bit of planning for this recipe, since you need to soak the cod for at least 24 hours, preferably for 2–3 days. The cod is then gently poached in milk and cut into tender shreds before being mixed with the mashed potatoes. The result is a tender and fluffy cod-potato mixture surrounded by a golden crunchy crust. Once the fritters are done, they reheat quite nicely in the oven. I often serve this as hors d'oeuvres with a side dish of tartare sauce, or as a main course with a green salad on the side.

675g (1lb 8 oz) salt cod

700ml (1¼ pints) milk, chilled

1 large floury potato, such as King Edward, Desiree
  or Maris Piper

sea salt and freshly ground black pepper

1 tablespoon finely chopped onion

2 garlic cloves, finely chopped

2 tablespoons chopped fresh parsley

4 large eggs, separated

1 tablespoon olive oil

½ teaspoon cayenne pepper

pinch of ground nutmeg

475ml (17fl oz) vegetable or rapeseed oil, for deep-frying

1   Trim away all the dark parts around the belly and tail of the cod, then rinse it in cold water and place it in a large container. Fill it with about 9.5 litres (2 gallons) cold water and refrigerate for 2–3 days. Change the water at least 3 times per day, and each time you change the water, rinse the container as well.

2   Place the cod in a medium saucepan. Cover with the cold milk and gently bring it to the boil over a medium heat. Reduce the heat to low and cook, uncovered, until it becomes opaque, about 5–7 minutes.

3   Using a slotted spoon, remove the cod and break the flesh with your hands into big chunks, then shred by either chopping it with a chef's knife or pulsing it through a food processor. You should end up with about 225g (8 oz) shredded fish. Place the cod in an airtight plastic container and refrigerate until ready to use (the cooked cod will keep for up to 6 hours).

4   Peel the potato and cut it into chunks. Place them in a heavy-based saucepan, cover with cold water and add a pinch of salt. Cover the pan, bring the water to the boil, then reduce the heat to medium and simmer until the potatoes are fork-tender, about 8–10 minutes. Drain them in a colander and, while they are still hot, pass them through a potato ricer or food mill.

5   In a large bowl, mix the shredded cod, mashed potatoes, onion, garlic, parsley, egg yolks, olive oil and cayenne. Add the nutmeg and salt and pepper to taste.

6   In a separate bowl, use an electric mixer fitted with the whisk attachment to beat the egg whites until they form soft peaks. Carefully fold the egg whites into the cod-potato mixture with a rubber spatula. You won't be able to shape the fritters with your hands, since the dough is so light, so you will need to spoon the batter directly into the hot oil.

7   Pour the vegetable oil into a heavy-based saucepan and heat the oil to 180°C/350°F, as measured with a deep-fat thermometer. If you don't have a thermometer, drip a little batter into the oil – when you hear a sizzling sound and see the batter turning golden brown, the oil is ready. Drop a tablespoonful of batter into the oil and only add as many as will fit without touching each other. Turn occasionally with a long slotted spoon, making sure all sides are browned evenly, about 2–3 minutes.

8   Remove each fritter from the oil and place it on a baking sheet lined with a double layer of kitchen paper to absorb any extra oil. Continue working in batches until all the fritters are cooked – keep the finished batches in a warm oven until serving. Serve hot – these can be reheated in a 150°C/300°F/Gas Mark 2 oven for 5–10 minutes.

QUAIL EGGS WITH KETCHUP SAUCE

Ovos de Codorna com Molho Rosé

It is very common in Brazilian restaurants to serve *couvert* (which usually consists of a basket of bread, assorted spreads and amuse-bouches) as soon as guests are seated at their table. One of my favourite foods of all the different types of *couverts* is quail eggs with red sauce. It's easy to make and very refreshing. The sauce can be prepared up to 3 days ahead of time.

SERVES 4

18 quail eggs
3 tablespoons mayonnaise
1 tablespoon plus 1 teaspoon crème fraîche
2 tablespoons double cream
¼ teaspoon lime juice
1 teaspoon tomato purée
2 tablespoons plus 1 teaspoon tomato ketchup
salt and freshly ground black pepper
3 tablespoons chopped fresh chives, to garnish

KETCHUP VINAIGRETTE

2 tablespoons tomato ketchup

2 tablespoons sherry or cidre vinegar

1 tablespoon finely chopped shallots

75ml (2½fl oz) extra virgin olive oil

1. In a bowl, mix together the ketchup, vinegar and shallots.

2. Add the olive oil, slowly, in a steady stream, whisking all the time until it creates an emulsion. This makes 125ml.

3. While Molho Rosé is the perfect expression of tradition when we are talking quail eggs, you might consider adding this vinaigrette to your repertoire as a lighter option. If you can't find maple vinegar, feel free to use apple cidre or sherry vinegar instead.

1. Place the eggs in a medium saucepan and cover with cold water. Place over a high heat and bring to the boil. Reduce the heat to low and simmer for 4½–5 minutes – you don't want to cook the yolks all the way through.

2. Using a slotted spoon, transfer the eggs to an ice bath. Let them chill until cool enough to touch, about 3 minutes. Peel each egg and place them in a bowl. Set aside.

3. Place the mayonnaise, crème fraîche, double cream, lime juice, tomato purée and ketchup in a bowl and whisk well until homogeneous. Season with salt and pepper.

4. Spoon some sauce on a plate and arrange the quail eggs on top. Sprinkle with the fresh chives.

RICE CROQUETTES WITH CAVIAR

Croquettes de Arroz com Caviar

While living in the United States, I heard about the rise of a chef named Alex Atala who is doing modern Brazilian cuisine at DOM, a restaurant located in São Paulo. I was not only happy to dine at DOM but proud to see a born and raised Brazilian chef praising our own ingredients with such towering ambition. The genius of his food is not its exotic flair but its clarity. One of Atala's simplest creations is the inspiration for this recipe. At DOM, it is topped with a small spoonful of caviar, and I suggest you follow suit. But even plain, the croquette is so good I am sure you'll munch on a few before the dollop of fish eggs.

MAKES 12–15 CROQUETTES

225g (8 oz) cooked white rice, cooled
55g (2 oz) freshly grated Parmesan
1 large egg
60ml (2fl oz) full-fat milk
40g (1 ½ oz) plain flour
sea salt and freshly ground black pepper
pinch of ground nutmeg
475ml (17fl oz) vegetable oil, for deep-frying
25–55g (1–2 oz) caviar

1. In a large bowl, mix together the rice, Parmesan, egg, milk and flour. Season with salt and pepper and the nutmeg. The batter should feel moist but firm. Using a tablespoon for portion control, form the batter into 12–15 croquette shapes.

2. Pour the vegetable oil into a heavy-based saucepan and heat to 180°C/350°F, as measured with a deep-fat thermometer. If you don't have a thermometer, drip a bit of batter into the oil – when you hear a sizzling sound and see the batter turning golden brown, the oil is ready. Fry the croquettes in batches. Add as many as will fit without touching each other. Turn occasionally with a long slotted spoon, making sure the croquettes are browned evenly on all sides.

3. Transfer to a baking sheet lined with a double thickness of kitchen paper to absorb any oil. Continue working in batches until all the croquettes are cooked. Keep the finished batches in a warm oven until serving.

4. Serve immediately. To reheat, place them in a 150°C/300°F/Gas Mark 2 oven until they are warm but not scorching hot, about 3–4 minutes.

MEAT CROQUETTES

Croquettes de Carne

On our way to our country house in Teresópolis, a city one hour from Rio, my family used to stop on the highway at a roadside place called Casa Do Alemão. People line up to eat their famous croquettes, which I have tried to replicate here. The recipe is quite simple and everything can be done ahead of time. You can make them small for hors d'oeuvres or a little bigger to be served as a main course with a green salad. The coating (flour, egg and crumbs) provides texture and keeps the oil from penetrating the filling during frying. To achieve successful dredging, none of the items should be overcoated. I even use a dry pastry brush to dust them off, ensuring a very thin layer of flour. Once coated in all three items, fry the croquettes immediately so that the coating remains dry. Take the beef mince out of the refrigerator 20–30 minutes before using so that it cooks more evenly and breaks into small bits of meat instead of bigger lumps.

225ml (8fl oz) veal stock (see page 113)

40g (1½ oz) unsalted butter

40g (1½ oz) plain flour

1 medium onion, diced

2 tablespoons olive oil

2 tablespoons finely chopped garlic

450g (1lb) beef mince

3 tablespoons tomato purée

1 teaspoon Worcestershire sauce

sea salt and freshly ground black pepper

1 teaspoon cayenne pepper

freshly grated nutmeg

2 large egg yolks

140g (5 oz) plain flour

2 large eggs, lightly beaten

125g (4½ oz) fresh breadcrumbs

475ml (17fl oz) rapeseed oil, for deep-frying

1   Pour the veal stock into a medium saucepan and bring it to the boil over a medium heat.

2   Meanwhile, in a different saucepan, melt the butter over a low heat.

3   Immediately add the flour to the butter and mix with a wooden spoon, cooking over a low heat, until the flour and butter become a roux, about 2 minutes. Add the veal stock all at once and cook, whisking constantly, until it thickens, about 3 minutes. Set aside.

4   In another saucepan, sauté the onion in the oil over a medium heat until they are soft and translucent, about 2 minutes. Add the garlic, and cook, while stirring, until it becomes hot, about another minute. Add the beef mince and break it up with the wooden spoon into tiny bits until it is completely cooked, about

3–5 minutes. Add the tomato purée and Worcestershire sauce and stir.

5   Pour in the reserved sauce and cook everything over a medium heat, stirring constantly, for about 2 minutes. Season with salt, pepper and nutmeg to taste and the cayenne, then add the egg yolks. Transfer to a flat tray and refrigerate for at least 2 hours, or overnight.

6   When the batter is completely cold, form it into 12–14 croquette shapes. Place the croquettes in a single layer in an airtight container and refrigerate for 1 hour.

7   Prepare 3 different trays: one for the flour, one for the eggs and one for the breadcrumbs. Pass each croquette through the flour, then the eggs, shaking the excess off each time. Coat them well with the breadcrumbs and shake off any excess.

8   Pour the vegetable oil into a heavy-based saucepan and heat the oil to 180°C/350°F, as measured with a deep-fat thermometer. If you don't have a thermometer, drip a bit of batter into the oil – when you hear a sizzling sound and see the batter turning golden brown, the oil is ready. Fry the croquettes in batches, only adding as many as will fit without touching each other. Turn occasionally with a long slotted spoon, making sure they are browned evenly on all sides, about 2–3 minutes.

9   Transfer to a baking sheet lined with a double thickness of kitchen paper to absorb any extra oil, then keep warm. Serve immediately with Red Pepper and Brazil Nut Pesto (page 26). These can be reheated in a 150°C/300°F/Gas Mark 2 oven for 5–10 minutes.

RED PEPPER AND BRAZIL NUT PESTO

Pesto de Pimentão Vermelho e Castanha-do-Pará

MAKES 350ML (12FL OZ)

75g (2¾ oz) shelled Brazil nuts

175g (6 oz) red pepper, peeled, deseeded
and cut into chunks

1 red bird's eye chilli (*pimenta malagueta*),
deseeded and cut into chunks (optional)

1 garlic clove

175ml (6fl oz) extra virgin olive oil

sea salt and freshly ground black pepper

⅛ teaspoon paprika

⅛ teaspoon ground chipotle chilli (optional)

1   Preheat the oven to 160°C/325°F/Gas Mark 3.

2   Place the nuts on a baking sheet and roast
them until they become fragrant, about
12 minutes. Remove from the oven and let
them cool completely at room temperature
before using.

3   Place the nuts, red pepper, chilli, if using,
garlic and about 1 tablespoon of the oil
in a food processor and process until
finely ground.

4   With the processor running, pour the
remaining oil in a thin, steady stream to
create an emulsion. Season with salt and
pepper and the paprika and chipotle, if using.

5   To serve, transfer the pesto to a bowl.
Pesto will keep in an airtight container in
the refrigerator for up to 3 days.

BAKED CHEESE CRACKERS

Sequilhos de Queijo

I learnt this recipe when I was 15 years old from Gracia Vienna, a cooking teacher from whom I took my first official cooking course in Rio. This recipe has remained a snacking mainstay for me ever since. I still love the taste of the beautiful golden cheese crust, the buttery flavour and the crumbles around the edges. I like to serve it on soups and salads or simply with a good glass of wine. Best of all, you can put the dough together in less than 5 minutes.

MAKES ABOUT 45 CRACKERS

200g (7 oz) plain flour, sifted
200g (7 oz) unsalted butter,
  cut into cubes, lightly chilled
½ teaspoon salt
100g (3½ oz) finely grated Parmesan
100g (3½ oz) finely grated Gruyère

1 Preheat the oven to 160°C/350°F/Gas Mark 3. Line a baking sheet with baking paper.

2 In a food processor, process the flour and butter until the dough begins to come together. Add the salt and cheeses and process everything until it is just blended, about 1 minute. Be wary of overworking the flour or incorporating air into the dough.

3 Transfer the mixture to a lightly floured surface and form it into a ball. Wrap it in clingfilm and refrigerate for at least 1 hour (or up to 3 days; you can also freeze the dough for up to 2 months).

4 Remove the dough from the refrigerator and, using a small ice-cream scoop or melon baller, make 2.5cm (1-inch) balls. Press each gently between the palms of your hands to flatten it just a little, as you would with a biscuit.

5 Arrange the crackers on the prepared baking sheet leaving a 2.5-cm (1-inch) space between them. Bake until the crackers are lightly golden brown, about 13–15 minutes, rotating the pan once.

6 Remove the sheet from the oven and transfer the crackers to a wire rack to cool. Eat slightly warm or at room temperature. Store the crackers in an airtight plastic container in the refrigerator for up to 5 days. To reheat them, place a batch on a baking sheet in a 180°C/350°F/Gas Mark 4 oven for 3–4 minutes.

PUMPKIN FLAN WITH DRIED BEEF SALAD

Flan de Abóbora com Salada de Carne Seca

Anyone who's ever eaten in a *botequim* has surely tasted *Purê de Abóbora com Carne Seca* – mashed pumpkin purée with dried beef. Seeking to lighten the dish and add a flash of luxe, I turned the recipe into a pumpkin flan topped with a warm *carne seca* salad and dressed with a pumpkin seed vinaigrette. This is quite easy to make and can be prepared ahead of time. Instead of pumpkin, you could use butternut squash or acorn squash. Just be sure you use a hard squash for this recipe.

SERVES 6–8

FOR THE FLAN

2 tablespoons rapeseed oil, for greasing
40g (1½ oz) unsalted butter
1 pumpkin (about 1.3kg/3 lb), peeled, seeded and cut into 2.5-cm/1-inch cubes
¼ teaspoon freshly grated nutmeg
⅛ teaspoon ground cinnamon
sea salt and freshly ground black pepper
5 garlic cloves, roughly chopped
4 large eggs
475ml (17fl oz) double cream

FOR THE MEAT

225g (8 oz) *carne seca* (dried beef)
1 small onion, peeled and halved
1 small carrot, peeled
1 celery stick

350ml (12fl oz) veal stock (see page 113)
1 plum tomato, peeled, deseeded and diced
25g (1 oz) frisée lettuce
2 tablespoons mayonnaise
2 tablespoons fresh chopped chives

FOR THE VINAIGRETTE

60ml (2fl oz) extra virgin olive oil
5 garlic cloves, finely chopped
40g (1½ oz) shelled unsalted pumpkin seeds
2 tablespoons sherry vinegar

pumpkin seed oil, to serve
6–8 125-ml (4-fl oz) ramekins or a muffin tin

1. Preheat the oven to 150°C/300°F/Gas Mark 2. Grease the ramekins lightly with the rapeseed oil.

2. Melt the butter in a large frying pan over a medium heat. Add the pumpkin and stir until all the pieces are hot and coated in butter. Add the nutmeg and cinnamon. Season lightly with salt and pepper. Cover the pan and reduce the heat to low. Cook, stirring occasionally. When the pumpkin is fairly soft, after about 5–7 minutes, add the garlic and stir. Cover and cook until the pumpkin and garlic are soft and tender, about 15–20 minutes. Close to the final minutes of cooking, uncover the pan to allow the excess moisture in the pumpkin to evaporate.

3. Transfer the pumpkin and garlic to a food processor fitted with the steel blade and process until smooth, about 1 minute. Add the eggs and double cream. Season with salt and pepper, pulsing to combine.

4. Ladle the custard into the ramekins. Set the ramekins in a shallow roasting tin, in the oven. Pour warm water into the tin until the sides of the ramekins are covered halfway. Bake until the custard is set, about 35–40 minutes.

5. Remove the roasting tin from the oven. Place the ramekins on a rack to cool to room temperature. Chill in the refrigerator for another 3 hours before unmoulding. You can prepare this up to 3 days ahead and store in the refrigerator, covered with clingfilm.

6. Meanwhile, prepare the meat. Trim any extra fat from the dried beef and soak it in cold water in the refrigerator for 24 hours, changing the water 3 times at regular intervals.

7. Place the meat in a medium saucepan and pour in enough fresh cold water to cover the meat by at least 5cm (2 inches). Bring the water to the boil, then replace the water with fresh cold again. Repeat this process 3 times.

8. Transfer the meat to another pan with the onion, carrot and celery. Cover everything with the veal stock. Simmer over a low heat, covered, until very tender, about 2 hours.

9. Remove the meat from the liquid and let it cool to room temperature. This can be done up to 2 days ahead; just leave the meat in the liquid, inside an airtight plastic container.

10. Using your hands, pull the meat into thin shreds and place it in a bowl. Discard any fat. Add the tomato, frisée lettuce, mayonnaise and chives and toss lightly.

11. To make the vinaigrette, place the olive oil in a small, heavy frying pan and cook the garlic and seeds over a low heat until the garlic starts to turn golden, about 2 minutes. Stir in the vinegar. Season with salt and pepper.

12. To serve, reheat the pumpkin flans in a 110°C/225°F/Gas Mark ¼ oven for 12–15 minutes. Unmould the flans by inverting each ramekin in the centre of a plate, arrange the meat salad on top of the flan and divide the vinaigrette sauce between the plates. Drizzle some pumpkin-seed oil around each flan and serve warm.

CARNE SECA

As Brazilians like to use a pressure cooker for everything, we often use one for carne seca, to make it soft and tender. Braising is a perfect alternative, and can be done up to 2 days ahead of time, but keep the meat in the braising liquid. If you cannot find carne seca, substitute any strong-flavoured smoked meat or even a country ham. As long as the shredded meat is full of flavour.

FLATBREAD TOPPED WITH VATAPÁ

In this recipe, the traditional Brazilian fish pureé *vatapá* (see page 78) finds a new role: sauce for a pizza. It can be spread just like tomato sauce on top of a flatbread, which is then topped with prawns, *dendê* (palm) oil, hearts of palm and tomatoes. This pizza-style preparation is a fun dish that is easy to prepare, great for entertaining, and surprisingly light. Making the flatbread is quite easy and it can be prepared ahead of time, but you could substitute ready-bought pizza dough. Just be sure to roll it very thinly, otherwise the dish will become too heavy.

FOR THE DOUGH

250g (9 oz) plain flour, sifted, plus extra
 for dusting
¼ teaspoon bicarbonate of soda
55g (2 oz) sea salt
4 tablespoons unsalted butter, cut into pieces
75ml (2½fl oz) cold water (a little more or a little less
 depending on humidity)
2 tablespoons olive oil

¼ recipe chilled Vatapá (see page 78)
1 vine tomato, thinly sliced
6 large raw prawns, peeled and deveined
40g (1½ oz) canned and drained hearts of palm, thinly sliced
3 tablespoons *dendê* (palm) oil
2 tablespoons chopped fresh coriander
sea salt and freshly ground black pepper

1   In the bowl of a food processor, combine the flour, bicarbonate of soda and salt. Add the pieces of butter and pulse until the mixture becomes a coarse meal.

2   With the machine running, add the water in a thin, steady stream. The dough will start to form into a ball. Before it actually holds its shape, turn the dough onto a lightly floured surface. Using your hands, gather the dough into a ball. If necessary, add a little more flour. Knead the dough by hand, or in a mixer fitted with the hook attachment, until the dough looks smooth, about 5 minutes.

3   Cut the dough in half and wrap each piece separately in clingfilm. Chill for at least 30 minutes in the refrigerator.

4   Preheat a gas barbecue or place a griddle pan over a medium-high heat.

5   On a lightly floured surface and using a rolling pin, roll one piece of dough into a 20-cm (8-inch) round, between 2–3mm (⅟₁₆–⅛ inch) thick, lifting the dough often and making sure the work surface and the dough are amply floured at all times. Wipe off the excess flour on top of the dough and brush the olive oil over the top side.

6   Carefully lift the dough, being sure to keep it in one piece, and place it with the olive oil side down on the grill or in the griddle pan. Using a pair of tongs, lift the dough to check for grill marks and that the dough is completely cooked on the bottom, about 2 minutes. Slide the dough onto a wire rack with the uncooked side up. Cool for 5–10 minutes.

7   Preheat the oven to 180°C/350°F/Gas Mark 4.

8   Spread the *vatapá* on top of the uncooked side, leaving a border of 1cm (½ inch) edge, as you would with a pizza. Arrange some tomato slices, hearts of palm and prawns on top. Season the entire surface with salt and pepper, then drizzle some *dendê* oil over it.

9   Bake the flatbread in the oven until the prawns are cooked and the flatbread is nice and crunchy, about 5–7 minutes.

10   Remove it from the oven and garnish with the coriander. Slice into 4–6 pieces and serve immediately.

BEAN FRITTERS
Acarajé

This fritter is probably the biggest symbol of African culture in Brazil. For over two centuries they have been sold in the streets of Bahia, a large state on Brazil's eastern coast, as a snack. *Acarajés* look like big oval meatballs with a reddish brown crust and a grainy soft bean purée on the inside, and one really is a meal in itself. I wanted to prepare this famous fritter in a smaller version while still keeping its authenticity. *Dendê*

(palm) oil (see Glossary on page 170) can be rather expensive, so I use half *dendê* and half rapeseed oil (if you use only rapeseed oil, the fritters won't achieve their beautiful reddish colour). The batter is prepared with uncooked beans, as they will cook when they are fried. If you use cooked or tinned beans, the batter will simply melt away in the oil. These *acarajés* can stand up to lots of hot seasoning.

175g (6 oz) dried black-eyed beans
1 small onion, diced
sea salt and freshly ground black pepper
pinch of cayenne pepper
pinch of Spanish paprika
475ml (17fl oz) rapeseed oil
475ml (17fl oz) *dendê* oil

1 Place the beans in a bowl and cover them with cold water.

2 Leave the beans to soak at room temperature uncovered, for at least 12 hours, preferably 24 hours, changing the water at least once (or any time you see that the water has turned brown). Discard any floating shells.

3 Drain the beans and spread them onto a baking sheet lined with kitchen paper so that they air-dry completely, about 5 minutes. Place the beans in the food processor with the onion. With the machine running, add some salt and black pepper and the cayenne and paprika and process until it is finely ground.

4 Pour the oils into a large heavy-based saucepan or casserole and heat the oil to 180°C/350°F, as measured with a deep-fat thermometer. If you don't have a thermometer, drip a bit of batter into the oil – when you hear a sizzling sound and see the batter turning golden brown, the oil is ready. Using 2 oval-shaped teaspoons, make little quenelles by scooping a bit of batter and transferring it from one spoon to another, putting some pressure against the spoons as you create the shape of a quenelle. Drop them directly into the hot oil. Only add as many as will fit in the oil without touching each other. Turn occasionally with a long slotted spoon, making sure all sides are browned evenly, about 3 minutes.

5 Transfer the fritters to a baking sheet lined with a double thickness of kitchen paper to absorb any extra oil. Continue working in batches until all the fritters are cooked. Keep the finished batches in a warm oven until serving. Serve immediately with a side of *Vatapá* (see page 78). These can be reheated in a 150°C/300°F/Gas Mark 2 oven for 5–10 minutes.

BLACK-EYED BEANS

Black-eyed beans, or black-eyed peas, are the original bean used in this recipe, but you could also use haricot beans. Be advised that the beans have to be soaked but cannot be pre-cooked. This recipe would not work with canned beans or cooked beans, as it would turn out too mushy.

YUCCA CROQUETTES

Croquettes de Aipim

Yucca is the most important of all vegetables in Brazil from a historical, cultural, economic and nutritional perspective. In this recipe, yucca is used as Mother Nature intended, raw and naked, and transformed into a crispy finger food – another *botequin* classic. The crunchy outside provides a nice contrast to the smoothness of the mashed yucca. The centre, filled with a small piece of blue cheese, pairs beautifully with the flavour of yucca. If you are not a fan of blue cheese, use another kind of cheese, such as Minas, goat's cheese, mozzarella, Parmesan, Manchego or provolone. Mashing yucca takes a bit more elbow work than mashing potatoes.

=== **MAKES ABOUT 20 CROQUETTES** ===

400g (2lb) yucca
40g (2½ oz) unsalted butter, softened
1 large egg yolk
sea salt and freshly ground black pepper
pinch of ground nutmeg
140g (5 oz) Gorgonzola, roughly crumbled

FOR THE COATING
140g (5 oz) plain flour
1 large egg, lightly beaten
175g (6 oz) panko breadcrumbs
475ml (17fl oz) rapeseed oil, for deep-frying

1 Cut off the ends of the yucca and make 3–4 vertical cuts from top to bottom with a paring knife. Peel the 2 layers of the vegetable: the brown skin and the inner white layer. Cut the yucca in half lengthways and remove the centre woody fibre with a paring knife. Cut the white flesh into 2.5-cm (1-inch) chunks.

2 Transfer the yucca to a medium saucepan, cover with fresh cold water by at least 2.5cm (1 inch) and add a good pinch of salt. Cover and bring to the boil. Reduce the heat to medium and cook until the yucca is tender, about 15–20 minutes.

3 Drain the yucca and, while still hot, pass through a food mill or potato ricer.

Immediately add the butter and egg yolk, mixing vigorously until well blended. Season with salt and pepper and the nutmeg.

4 Flour your hands. Form the mixture into tablespoon-sized balls. Gently press a dent into each ball and insert a small piece of cheese. Bring the dough up and around the cheese as you close and seal the edges. Shape the balls into croquettes. Flour your hands often and keep the cheese in the centre of each croquette.

5 Prepare 3 trays for the flour, egg and panko breadcrumbs. Pass the croquettes through each and shake off any excess.

6 Follow the deep-frying instructions (steps 8 and 9) for the Meat Croquettes on page 23.

FRIED EMPANADAS

Pastel de Carne Seca com Catupiry

MAKES ABOUT 20 EMPANADAS

225g (8 oz) *carne seca*
  (dried beef)
1 small onion, peeled
  and halved
1 small carrot, peeled
1 celery stick
350ml (12fl oz) veal stock
175g (6 oz) Catupiry cheese
1 litre (1¾ pints) vegetable
  oil, for deep-frying

FOR THE DOUGH
175g (6 oz) plain flour
1 teaspoon salt
¼ teaspoon baking
  powder
2 tablespoons extra
  virgin olive oil
60ml (2fl oz) plus 3 table
  spoons sparkling water
1 tablespoon vodka

From fillings of meat to cheese, seafood to poultry, the *pastel*, or empanada in English, is a treasured *botequim* food. In this recipe I use a very Brazilian filling of dried beef and *Catupiry* (see Glossary on page 170). In Brazil, there are several brands of ready-made dough available, and you can certainly find them in the UK. Any other braised meat can replace the *carne seca*. If you cannot find *Catupiry,* substitute cream cheese or a triple creamy cheese such as Saint André, Brie or Explorateur.

1   Prepare the dried beef as instructed in steps 6–10 on page 27. Then mix it with the Catupiry cheese in a bowl and set aside, or store in the refrigerator in an airtight plastic container for up to 2 days.

2   To prepare the dough, sift together the flour, salt and baking powder and place in the bowl of an electric mixer fitted with the paddle attachment.

3   Mix the olive oil, sparkling water and vodka in a separate bowl. Turn the machine on at low speed and pour the liquid over the dry ingredients in a steady stream, until the dough gathers into a ball and the side of the bowl is completely clean, about 1 minute.

4   Turn the machine off, change the attachment from a paddle to a hook and knead the dough until it's very smooth and elastic, about 10 minutes. Flour your hands and form the dough into a ball. Wrap it in clingfilm and chill for at least 30 minutes or up to 2 days. Bring the dough back to room temperature before proceeding.

5   Cut the dough in half and keep the piece you are not using wrapped in clingfilm to prevent it from drying out. On a lightly floured surface, roll the dough about 2mm (1/16 inch) thick. With a 7.5-cm (3-inch) round biscuit cutter, stamp out as many rounds as possible, about 6–8. Re-roll the scraps and stamp out more.

6   Working with one at a time, fill each round with 2 teaspoons of stuffing. Lightly brush the edges with water and fold the dough over into a half-moon shape. Crimp the edges with a fork to seal. Cover the assembled ones with clingfilm while you work on the other half of dough.

7   Deep-fry as per steps 8 and 9 on page 23.

YUCCA STICKS

Biscoito Palito de Polvilho

I grew up with an addiction to beach snacks. Among my favourites was *biscoito globo*, a round yucca cracker about the size and shape of a bagel. The flavour is quite mild, but it's the light crunchiness that draws munchers. These are sold in supermarkets in Brazil with lots of variety in shape but little in flavour. Recently, however, during one of my trips to Rio, I went to Claude Troisgrois's restaurant Olympe. He serves a fun and creative version of the cracker with a light touch of curry that is absolutely addictive. My experimentation with this recipe at home went through a few structural transformations, and finally my cracker became a stick. You can serve these as a snack or a light appetiser. Pair them with Red Pepper and Brazil Nut Pesto (see page 24) or another dip or spread and serve with a Caipirinha (see page 14). You can also substitute lemon zest for orange zest and thyme for rosemary. Although I use kosher salt inside the batter, feel free to use another kind of salt for sprinkling, such as sea salt.

200g (7 oz) sour manioc starch (*polvilho azedo*)

225ml (8fl oz) water

1 tablespoon full-fat milk

1 teaspoon sea salt, plus more for sprinkling

115g (4 oz) unsalted butter, softened at room
temperature

1 large egg

1 tablespoon plus 1 teaspoon chopped
fresh rosemary

finely grated zest of 1 orange

freshly ground black pepper

60ml (2fl oz) extra virgin olive oil

¼ teaspoon ground chipotle chilli, plus extra
for sprinkling

1 Preheat the oven to 180°C/350°F/Gas Mark 4. Line 2 baking sheets with baking paper.

2 Place the manioc starch in the bowl of an electric mixer fitted with the paddle attachment.

3 Bring the water, milk and salt to the boil in a small saucepan. Immediately pour the hot liquid over the manioc starch and beat at a low speed until the mixture looks like a coarse meal, about 1 minute. Add the butter and beat until the dough is smooth and the side of the bowl is clean. Add the egg, 1 tablespoon of the rosemary, orange zest and 2–3 twists of freshly ground black pepper. Beat the mixture until the dough turns pale and creamy, about 3–4 minutes.

4 Stop the machine and scrape the dough into a nylon piping bag fitted with a plain round nozzle, size number 3 (about ¼-inch diameter). Pipe the yucca sticks into 15-cm (6-inch) lengths onto the baking sheet, leaving about 1cm (½ inch) between each stick. It is important to pipe the sticks quite thinly, as they expand during baking time. (Alternatively, you can roll them by hand, on a surface lightly floured with manioc starch. Roll one piece at a time into a 15-cm (6-inch) long stick, then transfer them to the baking sheet.) Lightly brush the sticks with olive oil and sprinkle some salt, rosemary and a dusting of ground chipotle over each.

5 Bake them in the oven until they rise and turn slightly golden, about 25–35 minutes. Turn the oven off, open the door all the way and leave the sticks inside for another 30 minutes.

6 Remove the baking sheet from the oven and leave to cool for 10 minutes. Place the sticks in a tall glass and serve.

COOKING TIPS

A few little tricks you should follow to achieve success with this recipe: bake the sticks immediately after the dough is prepared, or the dough will dry out before baking and crack in the oven. Once they are baked and puffed, leave them inside the oven with the oven off and the door all the way open for at least 30 minutes. Otherwise, they will be hard like toffee. The more ventilation they receive, the crunchier they become, so if you have a convection mode in your oven, be sure to use it. Although these can be stored in a plastic container for 3–4 weeks, they tend to lose crunchiness with humidity and time, so before serving, reheat them in a 110°C/225°F/ Gas Mark ¼ oven for 20–25 minutes.

STUFFED CRAB SHELLS

Casquinha de Siri

In Brazil we have a different species of crab, but I think the American variety, especially the Maryland blue, is one of the best in the world – meatier and sweeter – and because of this I like to make this recipe more often in the United States than in Brazil. I love to serve this dish in a seashell. Most of the time, I use scallop shells instead of the original crab shells, but if you don't have sea creature shells available, just use a ceramic ramekin. This is a fantastic recipe for entertaining because it can be completely assembled ahead of time.

1 Place the bread in a bowl, pour the coconut milk over and leave to soak for 10–20 minutes while you prepare the other ingredients.

2 Pick over the crabmeat to remove any excess shell and set aside.

3 In a medium saucepan, warm the olive oil over a low heat. Add the onion and the yellow and green peppers and cook, stirring occasionally, until they are soft and tender. Add the garlic and cook for another minute, until it is tender. Add the tomatoes and cook for another minute until they are hot. Add the wine and reduce it by half, about 1–2 minutes. Add the bread and coconut milk and the dessicated coconut. Cook, stirring, until everything starts blending together, about 3 minutes.

MAKES 6–8 STUFFED SHELLS

2 slices white bread with crusts removed, diced
25ml (9fl oz) coconut milk
450g (1lb) fresh white crabmeat
2 tablespoons extra virgin olive oil
½ medium onion, chopped
about ⅔ yellow pepper, diced
about ⅔ green pepper, diced
3 garlic cloves, finely chopped
85g (3 oz) diced tomatoes
60ml (2fl oz) dry white wine
25g (1 oz) unsweetened dessicated coconut
1 teaspoon mustard
1 teaspoon fresh lemon juice
25g (1 oz) unsalted butter
2 tablespoons fresh chopped coriander
sea salt and freshly ground black pepper
¼ teaspoon Old Bay seasoning

FOR THE CRUST
2 tablespoons unsalted butter
85g (3 oz) manioc flour
sea salt and freshly ground black pepper
25g (1 oz) grated Parmesan
Maldon sea salt, to serve

4   Turn off the heat and add the crab, mustard and lemon juice. Fold everything together. Some pieces of crab will naturally shred, but try to keep some big lumps. Add the butter and coriander. Season with salt, pepper and the Old Bay. If your mixture looks dry, add 1–2 tablespoons coconut milk or wine. Transfer to a bowl and leave to cool completely. This can be done up to 2 days ahead and kept in an airtight container in the refrigerator.

5   Meanwhile, prepare the crust. Preheat the oven to 180°C/350°F/Gas Mark 4.

6   In a medium saucepan, melt the butter over a medium-low heat. Add the manioc flour and stir constantly, toasting the flour until it reaches a light golden colour. Watch carefully so that the flour does not burn. Transfer to a bowl and season with salt and pepper. Leave to cool for 5 minutes, then add the Parmesan and mix it in evenly.

7   Scoop the crab mixture into the scallop shells and repeat until all the filling is used. Spread a thin coat of crust on top. Place the shells on a baking sheet and bake in the oven until the filling is hot and the crust is a light golden brown, about 12–14 minutes.

8   To serve, place a small pile of Maldon sea salt on the bottom of a soup plate and place a shell on top.

PINEAPPLE MANCHEGO SKEWERS

Abacaxi picante com Manchego no palito

This is a very simple appetiser with an undeniable elegance, perfect for a last-minute get together. It's refreshing and perfectly balances the soft, sweet pineapple and the firm, nutty, salty Manchego – Spain's most famous sheep's milk cheese. In Brazil, I made this dish with Gouda, but once I tried it with Manchego, I never looked back. Look for an aged cheese, which will have a deep, buttery feel. To make a nice presentation, cut the fruit and the cheese into perfect squares of the same size. Save the trimmings for another recipe, or just snack on them like I do. Try to find some nice-looking skewers because this presentation relies on the sum of the very few parts. I like the bamboo ones sold in Asian stores.

MAKES ABOUT 20 SKEWERS

225g (8 oz) fresh pineapple, peeled and cored
175g (6 oz) Manchego, at room temperature
2 tablespoons sugar
25g (1 oz) salted butter
1 tablespoon water
⅛ teaspoon ground cinnamon
⅛ teaspoon ground chipotle chilli
sea salt and freshly ground black pepper
20 small bamboo skewers

CHOOSING CHEESE

This appetiser lends itself to many different types of cheese and is a great way to try something new, since you don't need to buy a lot. Cheeses that can be used instead of Manchego are Roncal or Zamorano from Spain, or Terrincho Velho from Portugal.

1 Cut the pineapple into 1-cm (½-inch) cubes using a serrated knife. Cut the Manchego into cubes about the same size. You should have about 20 pineapple cubes and 20 Manchego cubes.

2 Place the sugar in a small frying pan and add the water. Cook over a high heat until it turns into a light amber colour, about 2–3 minutes (since this a very small quantity it can be easily overcooked, so watch carefully).

3 Add the butter and swirl the pan around. Everything will splash and bubble, so be careful. When the butter is well blended with the caramelised sugar, turn the heat to low and add the cinnamon and ground chipotle. Cook the caramel until it becomes a little thicker, about 2 minutes.

4 Add the pineapple cubes and swirl the pan around, allowing the pineapple to caramelise in the sauce and become lightly golden brown, but being careful not to let it get too mushy, about 3–4 minutes. Season with salt and pepper.

5 Pour the pineapple and sauce onto a flat plate. While the fruit is still hot, place a piece of pineapple on the skewer, then a piece of Manchego. Place the skewers on a serving plate and serve immediately, while the pineapple is still warm.

CHICKEN FRITTERS
Coxinha de Galinha

Coxinha, 'little drumstick' in Portuguese, is a typical street food – the dough is stuffed with shredded chicken and Catupiry cheese, then deep fried. The 'little' label is inaccurate in my opinion. The old kitchens of Brazil make this delicious fritter too doughy and too big. One of my best friends and mentors, Patty Pulliam, shares my sentiments. A true connoisseur of Brazilian cuisine, she recently developed this ingenious recipe. It has all the grace of a *coxinha* and the finesse of a small appetiser: a crunchy and thin crust, a moist chicken filling and an elegant sauce. Patty suggests thigh meat for this recipe, it being the most succulent part of the chicken, but really you can use any leftover chicken. Traditionally, a pinch of turmeric is added to the dough.

MAKES 8–10 FRITTERS

FOR THE FILLING
1 tablespoon extra virgin olive oil
2 shallots, finely chopped
2 garlic cloves, finely chopped
1 bottled red pepper, drained and
    finely chopped
sea salt and freshly ground
    black pepper
150g (5½ oz) shredded cooked
    chicken, packed tight
1 tablespoon mayonnaise
3 tablespoons chopped
    fresh chives

FOR THE DOUGH
225ml (8fl oz) plus 2 tablespoons
    chicken stock
½ teaspoon extra virgin olive oil
1 teaspoon sea salt
⅛ teaspoon turmeric (optional)
140g (5 oz) plain flour, sifted,
    plus extra for dusting

FOR DREDGING
140g (5 oz) plain flour
2 large egg whites, lightly beaten
55g (2 oz) breadcrumbs
475ml (17fl oz) rapeseed oil, for frying

FOR THE CHEESE SAUCE
350ml (12fl oz) chicken stock
    (see page 112)
350g (12 oz) Catupiry cheese
sea salt and freshly ground black
    pepper
2 tablespoons chopped fresh chives
extra virgin olive oil, for drizzling

1   Warm the olive oil in a medium frying pan over a low heat. Add the shallots and cook them, stirring, until they are soft and translucent, about 1–2 minutes. Add the garlic and cook until it is hot, about 1 minute. Add the red pepper and season with salt and pepper. Transfer to a plate and leave to cool for about 10 minutes.

2   In a large bowl, place the shredded chicken and mix in the cooled shallot mixture, the mayonnaise and the chives. Season with salt and pepper. Leave to cool. (The filling can be prepared up to 1 day ahead and stored in an airtight plastic container in the refrigerator.)

3   Meanwhile, prepare the dough. In a medium saucepan, place the chicken stock, olive oil, salt and turmeric, if desired, and bring to a simmer over a low heat. When the stock is hot, add the flour all at once while stirring. A light crust will form on the bottom of the pan. Keep stirring – with vigour – for another minute to dry the dough.

4   Transfer the dough to an electric mixer fitted with the hook attachment and knead until it becomes soft and smooth, about 5 minutes. Scrape onto a floured surface and finish kneading the dough by hand, making sure your hands and the work surface are well floured. Form the dough into a flat disc and leave to rest at room temperature for 5–10 minutes before you start assembling the fritters.

5   Using a rolling pin, roll out the dough until it's about 3mm (⅛ inch) thick. Using a 9-cm (3½-inch) biscuit cutter, cut rounds of dough and place them on a baking sheet lined with baking paper. You will have some scraps that you can gather and re-roll. You should be able to make 8–10 rounds.

6   Using a tablespoon, scoop some filling into the centre of each round. To make the classic drumstick shape, using 2 lightly oiled hands, fold the dough up and around the filling into a beggar's purse and gently press the filling down into the centre as you close, pinching and sealing the edges. Pull the dough at the top out slightly so that it resembles a drumstick or an elongated chocolate kiss. Keep a moist cloth close at hand to clean your fingers each time they touch the filling. Make sure the dough is not cracked; if it does crack, wet your fingers in water and pinch the dough together.

7   Prepare 3 different trays for the flour, egg whites and breadcrumbs. Pass the fritters through each, shaking off any excess.

8   Pour the rapeseed oil into a heavy-based saucepan and heat to 180°C/350°F, as measured with a deep-fat thermometer. If you don't have a thermometer, dip a corner of a fritter into the oil – when you hear a sizzling sound, the oil is ready. Fry the fritters in batches. Turn occasionally with a long slotted spoon, making sure all sides are browned evenly, about 3–4 minutes.

9   Transfer to a baking sheet lined with a double thickness of kitchen paper to absorb any excess oil. Keep the finished batches in a warm oven until serving.

10   Prepare the cheese sauce. In a medium saucepan, bring the stock to a simmer over a low heat. Add the cheese and whisk it slowly and constantly until it melts completely. Season with salt and pepper.

11   Pour the sauce into a bowl and garnish with the chives and a drizzle of olive oil. Serve the fritters alongside.

KIBBE

Kibbe de Carne

Brazil is a melting pot that received an influx of immigrants in the mid-1900s, including Lebanese, who brought along all sorts of wonderful foods. Kibbe is one of them, and is a favourite of mine. For this recipe, make sure you buy very lean beef mince. If the meat is marbled with fat, the kibbe might not hold its shape when frying. Take the mince out of the refrigerator 20–30 minutes before using so that it blends more evenly with the bulghur. Bulghur wheat is a very nutritious grain and easy to work with. It has to soak in hot water before it is used, for 30 minutes or overnight in the fridge. If the bulghur has too much liquid after soaking, make sure you drain it and dry it, or the kibbes will be mushy. I like to shape these about 7.5cm (3 inches) long, but if you want to serve them as a main course, shape them a little larger. I love this accompanying Yogurt Mint Sauce, but feel free to serve them with other sauces, such as mustard sauce or chimichurri.

MAKES 45–50 KIBBES

175g (6 oz) bulghur wheat
450g (1lb) lean beef mince
1 small onion, finely chopped
2 spring onions (white and green parts), finely chopped
2 garlic cloves, finely minced
1 teaspoon dried oregano
3 tablespoons chopped fresh mint leaves
4 tablespoons extra virgin olive oil
2 teaspoons sea salt
freshly ground black pepper
pinch of cayenne pepper
few drops of Tabasco pepper sauce
475ml (17fl oz) rapeseed oil

1 Rinse the bulghur wheat with warm water to remove any dirt and excess starch. Drain it in a colander and place it in a bowl.

2 Meanwhile, bring 1 litre (1¾ pints) water to a boil and pour it over the bulghur. Cover the bowl with a tight lid or foil and leave to soak until the bulghur has expanded and tripled in size, 45 minutes–1 hour.

3 Place the beef mince in a large bowl. Add the soaked bulghur wheat, then stir in the onion, spring onion, garlic, oregano, mint and olive oil. Mix well with your hands until the mixture is well blended. Season with the salt, pepper, cayenne and Tabasco sauce and mix again.

4   Start forming oval shapes by first rolling a tablespoon of mixture in a circular motion between the palms of your hands, then forming two pointed ends. (You can store the kibbes in an airtight container in the refrigerator for 1 day. Make sure you bring to room temperature at least 30 minutes before frying.)

5   Pour the rapeseed oil into a heavy-based saucepan or casserole and heat the oil to 180°C/350°F, as measured with a deep-fat thermometer. If you don't have a thermometer, dip one kibbe into the oil – when you hear a sizzling sound, the oil is ready. Fry the kibbes in batches. Only add as many as will fit without touching each other. Turn occasionally with a long slotted spoon, making sure they are browned on all sides, about 3–5 minutes.

6   Transfer to a baking sheet that's been lined with a double thickness of kitchen paper to absorb any excess oil. Continue working in batches until all the kibbes are fried. Keep the finished batches in a warm oven until serving. Serve immediately. These can be reheated in a 150°C/300°F oven for 5–10 minutes.

YOGURT MINT SAUCE

MAKES 225ML

125ml (4fl oz) natural low-fat Greek yogurt
125ml (4fl oz) soured cream
1 tablespoon Dijon mustard
1 tablespoon finely chopped red onion
a few drops of freshly squeezed lemon juice
a few drops of Tabasco sauce
sea salt and freshly ground black pepper
2 tablespoons chopped fresh mint

1   In a medium bowl, whisk together the yogurt, soured cream and mustard.

2   Stir in the red onion, lemon juice and Tabasco sauce.

3   Season with salt and pepper.

4   Add the mint and fold it in with a spatula. This sauce can be prepared up to 3 days in advance.

Salads and Soups
Sopas e Saladas

CRUNCHY MINAS CHEESE WITH TOMATO AND PESTO

Salada de Minas Crocante com Tomate e Pesto Brasileiro

Minas cheese is the muse cheese of Brazil. Originally from the state of Minas Gerais, hence the name, this pure white-coloured cheese has an incredible farm freshness, and a very humble pedigree, considering its popularity. The taste is a cross between a feta, ricotta and mozzarella. Like other fresh white cheeses, Minas has a way of complementing other flavours without masking them. See the Glossary on page 170 for more on Minas cheese. For this recipe, Minas cheese is covered in a panko crust, cooked in olive oil until it becomes lightly golden brown and paired with tomato bruschetta and Brazilian pesto. If you can't find Minas cheese, you can use another white cheese, such as *ricotta salata*, *queso blanco* or even goat's cheese. The tomato can be prepared a few hours ahead, but the cheese should not be coated and cooked until just before serving. During the summer months, serve this with gorgeous heirloom tomatoes or even with just a fresh green salad and a good vinaigrette.

SERVES 6–8

140g (5 oz) Brazil nuts
1 whole garlic clove, peeled, plus 2 cloves, finely chopped
20g (¾ oz) fresh flat-leaf parsley
20g (¾ oz) fresh coriander
185ml (6½fl oz) extra virgin olive oil
sea salt and freshly ground black pepper
pinch of cayenne pepper
6 plum tomatoes, peeled and deseeded
1 large shallot, finely chopped
70g (2½ oz) plain flour
1 large egg, lightly beaten
85g (3 oz) panko breadcrumbs
450g (1 lb) Minas cheese
225ml (8fl oz) olive oil
225–280g (8–10 oz) rocket leaves, to garnish

1 Preheat the oven to 160°C/325°F/Gas Mark 3.

2 Roast the nuts on a baking sheet until they just start to develop an aroma, about 12 minutes. Remove from the oven, transfer to a plate and cool completely. Rub the nuts between your hands or use a cloth to remove the thin brown skins. They should come off quite easily.

3 Place the nuts, garlic clove, herbs and 60ml (2fl oz) of the olive oil in a food processor. Pulse until blended. With the machine running, add the remaining olive oil (save

1 tablespoon) in a steady stream. Season with salt, pepper and the cayenne. Store in an airtight container in the refrigerator for up to 3 days.

4   Chop the tomatoes and place them in a bowl. Mix in the shallot and finely chopped garlic. Season well with salt and pepper. Drain out the tomato juices. Transfer the tomatoes to a bowl, add the 1 tablespoon olive oil and mix with a rubber spatula.

5   Prepare 3 different trays for the flour, egg and panko breadcrumbs.

6   Cut the Minas cheese into 1-cm (½-inch) slices, then, using a 5-cm (2-inch) biscuit cutter, cut rounds out of the cheese. Pat the cheese dry with kitchen paper. Pass

each piece of cheese through the flour, egg and breadcrumbs, shaking off the excess in between.

7   Heat the olive oil for frying in a large sauté pan over a medium heat. Carefully add the cheese rounds and cook on each side until lightly golden brown, about 2 minutes per side. Using a fish slice, remove the cheese rounds from the pan and transfer them to a plate or a baking sheet lined with a double sheet of kitchen paper.

8   To serve, place a mound of tomatoes on a plate, drizzle pesto sauce around it and top with a warm Minas cheese round. Garnish with a few rocket leaves.

GRIDDLED MINAS CHEESE WITH A BRAZILIAN PESTO SAUCE

Minas Grelhado com Pesto Brasileiro

This glorious appetiser requires very little work. The cheese is cooked but its firm texture keeps it from melting completely. Make sure you buy the whitest and freshest Minas cheese so that the griddled marks appear, and try to use a griddle pan or barbecue grill with a small grill elevation to prevent the cheese sticking to the surface. Cutting the cheese into triangles gives this dish a fancier look, but if you don't want to spare any cheese, leave it in the original round shape and enjoy those extra few nibbles. A combination of Brazil nuts with parsley and coriander give this pesto a Brazilian wallop that is charming but not overwhelming.

| SERVES 4–6 |

FOR THE PESTO SAUCE
50g (1¾ oz) Brazil nuts
1 garlic clove, peeled
20g (¾ oz) fresh flat-leaf parsley
20g (¾ oz) fresh coriander leaves
175ml (6fl oz) extra virgin olive oil
pinch of cayenne pepper
sea salt and freshly ground black pepper

400g (14 oz) firm Minas cheese
2 tablespoons extra virgin olive oil

1   Preheat the oven to 160°C/325°F/Gas Mark 3.

2   Prepare the pesto as per the instructions on pages 46–47.

3   Place a griddle pan over a high heat on the hob, or preheat a gas barbecue.

4   Trim the round Minas cheese into a square. Cut the cheese in half diagonally to make 2 large triangles. Cut each large triangle in sections to make 4–5 thinner triangles, about 1cm (½ inch) thick. Brush each triangular slice with the olive oil and season with just a tiny pinch of salt (not too much, since Minas cheese is already salted) and pepper.

5   Grill the cheese until you see medium-brown grill marks on both sides, being careful not to let the cheese melt, about 2 minutes on each side. Carefully transfer each triangle to a serving platter.

6   Spoon the pesto (which should be slightly cold or at room temperature) over the cheese and serve immediately.

CHICKEN SALAD WITH STRING POTATOES

Salpicão de Frango

The best part of this salad is that it's an extraordinary dish from very ordinary kitchen ingredients: chicken, carrots, onions, potatoes, tomato sauce and raisins. With the right treatment to each one of them, they become a chicken salad like you've never had before. You'll need a whole chicken for this recipe, but you can also adapt the recipe if you have left-over chicken. Try to resist cutting the chicken with a knife when you pull it from the carcass. It's the textural juxtaposition of the hand-pulled chicken mixed with the carrots and crunchy potatoes that takes this dish to the next level. The thinner you pull the chicken, the better it will taste. Did I mention that you can make everything ahead of time? And the variations are endless – after Christmas, try making it with turkey and cranberry.

SERVES 6–8

2 floury potatoes, such as Desiree or Maris Piper

1 litre (1¾ pints) vegetable oil, for deep-frying

salt

1 whole, ready-roasted chicken, 1.3–1.8kg (3–4lb)

2 tablespoons olive oil

1 large onion, thinly sliced

115g (4 oz) raisins

2 tablespoons white wine

115g (4 oz) mayonnaise

3 tablespoons pasta tomato sauce, preferably marinara

2 tablespoons chopped fresh parsley

sea salt and freshly ground black pepper

⅛ teaspoon cayenne pepper

⅛ teaspoon paprika

4–5 carrots, coarsely grated

1   Cut the potatoes into juliennes, using a mandoline, or do it by hand. Place the potatoes in a bowl of cold water as you cut them, but change the water at least once, washing away any starch. Spread the potatoes onto a baking sheet lined with kitchen paper, and let them air-dry for 5 minutes.

2   Pour the oil into a large, heavy-based saucepan and heat to 180°C/350°F, as measured on a deep-fat thermometer. If you don't have a thermometer, dip one potato into the oil – when you hear a sizzling sound, the oil is ready. Fry the potatoes in batches until they are lightly golden brown. Transfer to a plate lined with a double thickness of kitchen paper and immediately season with table (not sea) salt. Set aside. You can prepare the potatoes up to a day ahead; just be sure to keep them in an airtight plastic container at a dry room temperature.

3   To prepare the salad, pull the meat off all parts of the chicken by hand. (Discard the bones or use them for a chicken stock.) The thinner the meat, the better. You should have about 600g (1lb 5 oz) chicken. Set aside.

4   Place the olive oil in a large frying pan and cook the onion over a low heat, stirring occasionally, until soft and translucent, about 10–15 minutes. (Resist the temptation to turn the heat to high, otherwise the onion will brown.) Transfer to a bowl and set aside.

5   In a small saucepan, cook the raisins in the wine over a low heat, just until the raisins are soft, about 3–5 minutes. Transfer the raisins with any remaining wine to a plate to cool and set aside.

6   In a medium bowl, mix together the mayonnaise and tomato sauce. Season with salt and pepper and the cayenne and paprika.

7   In a big bowl, mix together the chicken, onion, raisins, carrots and mayonnaise sauce. Taste to adjust the seasoning. You can store the salad in an airtight plastic container in the refrigerator for up to 2 days. Just remember to bring it to room temperature 20–30 minutes before serving.

8   Place the chicken salad on a large platter and arrange the string potatoes on top. For a fancier presentation, use individual ring moulds, and press the salad inside. Remove the ring and garnish with the potatoes on top.

ROAST CHICKEN

If you prefer to roast your own chicken, preheat the oven to 200°C/400°F/Gas Mark 6. Season the chicken with salt and pepper, and place it in a roasting pan. Roast in the oven until it's done (the breast should be cooked to about 68°C/155°F and the legs to about 74°C/165°F, both as measured by a meat thermometer, about 40–45 minutes, or until the juices run clear when a skewer is inserted into the thickest part of the meat. Remove the chicken from the oven, cut the trussing string off and wait until the chicken cools to room temperature before pulling the meat from the carcass.

SALTED AND PEPPERED MELON

Melão com Sal e Pimenta, Molho de Manga e Pimentão Amarelo

A perfect piece of melon that I enjoyed on a hot day in Rio is the inspiration for this recipe. Sweet and juicy melon marries quite well with savoury foods and it takes the pepper and fleur de sel right in. The mango and yellow pepper sauce is a perfect complement to the lushness of the melon. The orangey-pink flesh of the cantaloupe and its firm, creamy texture make it the perfect melon to receive a quick sear in the frying pan. However, the abundance of melons available today are too varied to lock you onto only one kind, so feel free to use other types of melons. But be careful when choosing melons, especially when they have been transported over a long distance. I've been quite disappointed at times with rock-hard melons that are practically tasteless. So be sure to make this recipe when good melons are in season during the summer.

SERVES 4–6

4 tablespoons extra virgin olive oil
1 small shallot, chopped
1 yellow pepper, deseeded and chopped
1 ripe mango, cut into small chunks
350ml (12fl oz) chicken stock (see page 112)
1 ripe small melon, 900–1.1kg (2–2lb 8 oz)
sea salt and freshly ground black pepper
fleur de sel
40g (1½ oz) lamb's lettuce, washed and dried

1 Heat 2 tablespoons of the olive oil in a medium saucepan over a medium heat. Add the shallot and yellow pepper and cook, stirring occasionally, until they are soft and the shallot is translucent, about 3 minutes. Add the chicken stock and bring to a simmer. Cook until reduced by half, about 5–6 minutes. Add the mango chunks and cook until they are hot and mushy, about 2 minutes. Season lightly with salt and pepper.

2 Transfer to a blender and blend until smooth. Strain the sauce through a fine sieve directly into a bowl. Set aside. The sauce can be prepared up to 3 days ahead of time and stored in an airtight plastic container in the refrigerator.

3   Using a sharp knife, trim the skin from the melon. Cut it in half lengthways and scoop out the seeds. Slice each half lengthways into 4–5 wedges to make a total of 8–10 wedges, depending on the size of the fruit. Each wedge should be about 2.5–4cm (1–1½ inches) thick. Season one side only with pepper.

4   In a large frying pan, heat the remaining 2 tablespoons of olive oil over a high heat. Add a few melon wedges, and cook on the peppered side only until a nice caramelised crust develops. Don't crowd the pan. If necessary, cook the wedges in batches. Using tongs, carefully transfer the wedges to a platter. Sprinkle a few crystals of fleur de sel onto each spear on the seared side of the melon.

5   Place 2 wedges of melon on each plate with the seared side up, and carefully drizzle the mango sauce, which should be served at room temperature or slightly chilled, around the spears. Arrange a mound of lamb's lettuce on the plate and lightly drizzle with olive oil and season with salt.

MANGO, SMOKED SALMON, AND ROCKET SALAD

Salada de Manga e Salmao Defumado com Rúcula

This recipe is inspired by a dish I used to make when I worked at La Caravelle, one of New York City's greatest temples of French haute cuisine. At that time, the young and talented chef Cyril Renaud prepared a smoked salmon and mango napoleon layered with crème fraîche that was so naturally sweet and refreshing that it always made me think of Brazil. Here, I use the same key ingredients in a salad. The buttery slices of sweet mango are inserted between salty smoked salmon and arranged over a bed of peppery rocket, then topped with a simple and tangy vinaigrette sauce. In each bite you can taste the contrast of sweet, salty and peppery, making this salad intensely flavoured and quite elegant.

2 tablespoons freshly squeezed lemon juice

1 teaspoon Dijon mustard

1 tablespoon crème fraîche

75ml (2½fl oz) extra virgin olive oil

1 tablespoon rapeseed oil

1 medium ripe mango, peeled, stoned and cut into thin slices

140g (5 oz) thinly sliced smoked salmon, cut into strips

5 ounces baby rocket leaves

sea salt and freshly ground black pepper

1   Place the lemon juice, mustard and crème fraîche in a food processor or blender. Pulse until well blended.

2   Mix the two oils in a measuring jug, then with the processor running, pour in a steady stream into the crème fraîche mixture. Season with salt and pepper. This vinaigrette can be prepared up to 3 days ahead of time and stored in an airtight plastic container in the refrigerator.

3   Just before serving, place the rocket in a large bowl and pour just enough dressing over the leaves to coat and toss. Be careful not to overdress the leaves, or they will turn mushy quite fast.

4   Place the rocket leaves on individual serving dishes and arrange the slices of mango and salmon on top. Lightly drizzle more vinaigrette on top and serve immediately. Store any extra vinaigrette in an airtight plastic container in the refrigerator for up to 1 week.

MANGO

The mango is an exceptional fruit, full of pulp, flavour, aroma, texture, juice and sweetness. It is the second most consumed tropical fruit, after the banana. The mango tree originated in India and was first brought to Europe, Africa and the Americas by Portuguese explorers in the 18th century. The tree adapted particularly well to the climate of Brazil. Today, mangos are available in most supermarkets. There are over 500 varieties of mangos but those that are available all year round are Kent, Keitt and Tommy Aitkins. Feel free to use any kind of mango for this salad, as long as the fruit is perfectly ripe (it should feel slightly soft when pressed with your thumb); it pairs splendidly with the smoked salmon and rocket.

CURRIED CHICKEN SALAD

Salada de Galinha ao Curry com Amêndoas e Passas

Chicken salad is an American staple and a Brazilian one, too. This salad is among the most flavourful approaches to the classic that you'll find, whether you use leftover chicken or with meat cooked just for this purpose. The presence of almonds, sultanas and cooked onion with curry powder and turmeric adds both crunchy and sweet elements to the chicken salad. It makes a great buffet dish or a small lunch served with a green salad on the side, and it's quite easy to prepare. Although you can make this recipe in just half an hour, it tastes even better the next day. I have been making this dish for about 15 years and I still get asked for the recipe every time I make it.

MAKES 2 TO 4 SERVINGS

55g (2 oz) golden raisins

2 tablespoons white wine

½ small onion, finely diced

1 tablespoon olive oil

2 garlic cloves, finely chopped

1 teaspoon curry powder

1 teaspoon turmeric

225ml (8fl oz) chicken stock

225g (8 oz) cubed cooked chicken
 (light and dark meat)

50g (1¾ oz) almonds, lightly toasted and
 roughly chopped

3 tablespoons mayonnaise

1 tablespoon shop-bought balsamic vinaigrette

sea salt and freshly ground black pepper

2 tablespoons chopped fresh parsley, to garnish

1 Cook the sultanas in the wine in a small saucepan over a low heat just until they are soft, about 3–5 minutes. Transfer the sultanas with any remaining wine to a plate to cool and set them aside.

2 In a small sauté pan over a low heat, cook the onion in the olive oil, stirring occasionally, until soft and translucent, about 2–3 minutes. Add the garlic, curry powder and turmeric and continue stirring and cooking until they are hot, about 1 minute. Add the chicken stock and cook at a low simmer, letting it reduce by 80 per cent, for about 5 minutes. Be sure to not to let the onion dry out. While still wet, transfer the curried onion to a plate and leave to cool to room temperature.

3 In a big bowl, mix the sultanas, curried onion, chicken, almonds, mayonnaise and balsamic vinaigrette. Mix everything together until the salad is well blended.

4 Season with salt and pepper. At this point you can either serve immediately or store in an airtight plastic container in the refrigerator for up to 3 days. Serve sprinkled with the chopped parsley garnish.

BRAZILIAN CHICKEN SOUP

Canja de Galinha

Some dishes are universal, with a slight regional variation. Matzo ball soup, chicken noodle soup, wonton soup – whether it's Jewish, American or Chinese, all of these dishes are comforting. Here is the Brazilian version. This soup is so simple that it inspired a slang word in Portuguese: when something is 'Canja' it means it is easy. The basic ingredients are chicken, rice and *mirepoix* (onions, celery and carrots). I like to add some asparagus in the springtime. Cook the chicken gently without letting it come to the boil, to create a meat that is succulent and tender. I love how the rice infuses the soup with starch and the chicken skin infuses the liquid with natural fat. I love to eat this soup with the cheese crackers on page 25.

cheese crackers on page 25.

SERVES 6–8

1 whole chicken, 1.6kg (3lb 8 oz)
sea salt and freshly ground black pepper
700ml (1¼ pints) chicken stock
3 carrots, peeled and thinly cut on the diagonal
3 celery sticks, thinly cut on the diagonal
1 onion, thinly sliced
200g (7 oz) white long-grain rice
8 asparagus spears, thinly cut on the diagonal

1 Wash the chicken well with cold water, making sure to clear the inside cavity removing any liquid and organs from the chicken. Season with salt and pepper and place in a large flameproof casserole. Cover with chicken stock, add 700ml–1 litre water and cover with the lid. Bring to the boil over a medium to high heat and skim off any foam that may form. Reduce the heat to low and gently simmer, covered, until the chicken is cooked through, about 25–35 minutes (remember, don't let it boil at any point).

2 Using a pair of tongs, remove the chicken from the water, shaking any liquid from the chicken into the pan, and transfer to a plate. Cool to room temperature.

3 Add the carrots, celery, onion and rice to the liquid. Lightly season with salt and pepper and simmer over a low heat until the vegetables are tender and the rice is cooked through, about 15–20 minutes.

4 Meanwhile, pull the chicken meat into thin shreds and add to the soup. Discard the bones (or save them for stock) and skin.

5 A few minutes before serving, add the asparagus to the soup and simmer until just cooked, about 3–4 minutes. Taste the soup, season again if necessary with salt and pepper and serve hot.

PORTUGUESE SOUP
Caldo Verde

This classic soup is a full meal in itself, satisfying in every season. In Portugal they like to use a very green cabbage called *couve gallego*, but in Brazil this soup became a classic using *couve mineira*, otherwise known as collard greens. You can substitute spring greens or use curly kale. Some recipes call for starchy potatoes, like the King Edward, Desiree or Maris Piper variety, which are then puréed with

the chicken stock. But I think a young potato adds a more delicate flavour and I prefer to smash just a tiny portion of potatoes. It will all depend on the quality of chicken stock you are using. If your stock is very watery, thickening the soup by smashing some of the potatoes will do well. If your stock is nice and thick, that won't be necessary. In either case, this soup is easy to prepare and quite nourishing.

4 tablespoons olive oil

1 large onion, diced

3 garlic cloves, finely chopped

550g (1lb 4 oz) small, waxy yellow-fleshed
   potatoes, peeled and cut into 1-cm (½-inch) chunks

1.4 litres (2½ pints) chicken stock

350g (12 oz) pork sausage (linguica or chorizo,
   see Glossary on page 170)

225g (8 oz) spring greens or curly kale

sea salt and freshly ground black pepper

pinch of cayenne pepper

1   Place 3 tablespoons of the olive oil and the
    onion in a large saucepan, over a low heat, and
    cook until soft, stirring occasionally, about 5–7
    minutes. Add the garlic and cook until hot,
    about 1 minute. Add the potatoes and cook,
    stirring occasionally, until they are hot, about
    4 minutes. Add the chicken stock. Cover
    the pan and bring the soup to the boil, then
    lower the heat and simmer gently until the
    potatoes are just cooked and fork-tender,
    about 15 minutes.

2   In the meantime, add the remaining
    tablespoon of olive oil to a medium sauté
    pan and sauté the sausages, turning
    frequently, until they are nicely browned on
    all sides, about 5 minutes. Transfer to a flat
    plate lined with kitchen paper.

3   Scoop out 2 tablespoons of the potatoes,
    place them on a plate and mash them
    completely with a fork. Return the mashed
    potatoes to the soup. Remember, the
    amount of potatoes you mash and add
    will affect how thick the soup will be.

4   When the sausages are cool enough to
    handle, cut into slices a little thinner than
    1cm (½ inch). Add them to the soup, cover and
    cook at a gentle simmer for 5 minutes.

5   In the meantime, trim the thick stems from
    each leaf of the spring greens or kale and cut
    the leaves into fine shreds. Add the greens
    and cook at a gentle simmer for another
    5 minutes. If you want to prepare the soup
    ahead of time, set the greens aside and add
    them 5 minutes before serving, as they are
    what will establish the bright green colour
    that gives *caldo verde* its name.

6   Season the soup with salt and pepper and
    the cayenne. Serve in deep soup bowls.

CHICKEN STOCK

Making chicken stock can be quite
impractical. However, stock can be
part of your cooking on a semi-
regular basis by simply using the
leftover trimmings of a chicken. I
never throw away carcasses from
roasted chickens because they make
an excellent stock and it freezes very
well. Some supermarkets, butchers and
delicatessens sell fresh stock – that
should be your second-best option. If
bouillon powder or stock cubes are
your only option, no problem, the
soup is still well worth making. Just be
careful when seasoning, as they tend
to be saltier then fresh stock. See page
112 for a stock recipe.

YUCCA AND COCONUT SOUP WITH SCALLOPS

Sopa de Aipim e Côco com Vieiras

One of the most rewarding aspects of cooking is creating new recipes by taking flavours that work well in a classic dish and cooking them with another technique. With this soup I rethought the flavour combination of yucca and coconut. This combination could not be more classically Brazilian, but it is rarely served as a soup. The yucca really strikes an earth tone in a way that no other root vegetable can achieve. The coconut milk adds a creamy texture that comes without any cream at all. The delicacy of scallops must, of course, not be overcooked. And, finally, it is so easy to prepare.

SERVES 4

2 tablespoons *dendê* (palm) oil (see Glossary)

1 medium onion, diced

3 garlic cloves, roughly chopped

15g (½ oz) fresh root ginger, peeled and roughly chopped

1 yucca, prepared (see page 32)

3 plum tomatoes, quartered

60ml (2fl oz) dry white wine

775ml (1⅓ pints) chicken stock (see page 112)

225ml (8fl oz) coconut milk

1 tablespoon tomato purée

sea salt and freshly ground black pepper

225g (8 oz) shelled uncooked scallops

2 tablespoons extra virgin olive oil

2 tablespoons chopped fresh chives, to garnish

1   In a medium saucepan, heat the *dendê* oil (palm oil) over a low heat and add the onion. Cook, stirring occasionally, until it becomes soft and translucent, about 3–5 minutes. Add the garlic and ginger and stir. Add the yucca, stirring until it is hot, about 2 minutes. Add the tomatoes and stir well. Add the wine and reduce almost completely.

2   Add the chicken stock, coconut milk and tomato purée and stir well. Season with salt and pepper and bring to a simmer, uncovered, over medium to high heat. Reduce the heat to low, cover and simmer gently until the yucca is completely cooked, about 15–20 minutes.

3   Working in batches, purée the soup in a blender. As each batch of soup is puréed, pour it directly into a sieve set over another saucepan. Discard the solids. Season the soup with salt and pepper.

4   Pat the scallops dry and season with salt and pepper. Cook them in the olive oil in a medium sauté pan over a medium heat until they just start to turn opaque, about 2 minutes.

5   Reheat the soup if necessary and ladle it into warm bowls. Divide the scallops between each and garnish with the chopped chives.

PUMPKIN AND COCONUT SOUP

Sopa de Abóbora com Côco

SERVES 4–6

2 tablespoons extra virgin olive oil

1 pumpkin, about 1.3kg (3lb), peeled, deseeded
   and cut into 1-cm (1-inch) cubes

3 small carrots, roughly chopped

sea salt and freshly ground black pepper

2 onions, roughly chopped

4 garlic cloves, roughly chopped

175ml (6fl oz) white wine

700ml–1 litre (1¼–1¾ pints) chicken stock

475ml (17fl oz) coconut milk

25g (1 oz) butter

2 tablespoons freshly chopped chives, to garnish

Like peas and carrots, pumpkins and coconuts are great pals. This very Brazilian partnership is traditionally seen in sweets and pastries, especially in jams sold in glass jars. I use it as another source of inspiration for a simple and casual soup. In terms of technique, it is similar to the classic American pumpkin soup, but the coconut milk adds a creamy and tropical flavour that elevates the pumpkin. If you'd like to add some texture, feel free to garnish with lightly toasted pumpkin seeds or lightly toasted coconut, or both.

1   In a medium saucepan, heat the olive oil over a medium heat and add the pumpkin and carrots. Season very lightly with salt and pepper and cook, stirring occasionally, until they start to soften, about 5 minutes. Be careful that they don't turn brown.

2   Add the onions and continue to cook, stirring occasionally, until they start to soften, about 3 minutes. Add the garlic and let it get hot, about 1 minute. Add the white wine and let it reduce almost completely, about 3 minutes.

3   Add the chicken stock and bring to the boil. Add the coconut milk and bring to the boil again. Season lightly with salt and pepper and reduce the heat to low. Cover the pan and gently simmer the soup until the pumpkin and carrots are completely cooked, about 15–20 minutes.

4   Remove the pan from the heat. Working in batches, purée the soup in a blender. As each batch of soup is puréed, pour it directly into a sieve set over another saucepan. Discard the solids. Add the butter and whisk well. Taste the soup and adjust the seasoning with salt and pepper.

5   Garnish with the chives and serve with the Baked Cheese Crackers on page 25.

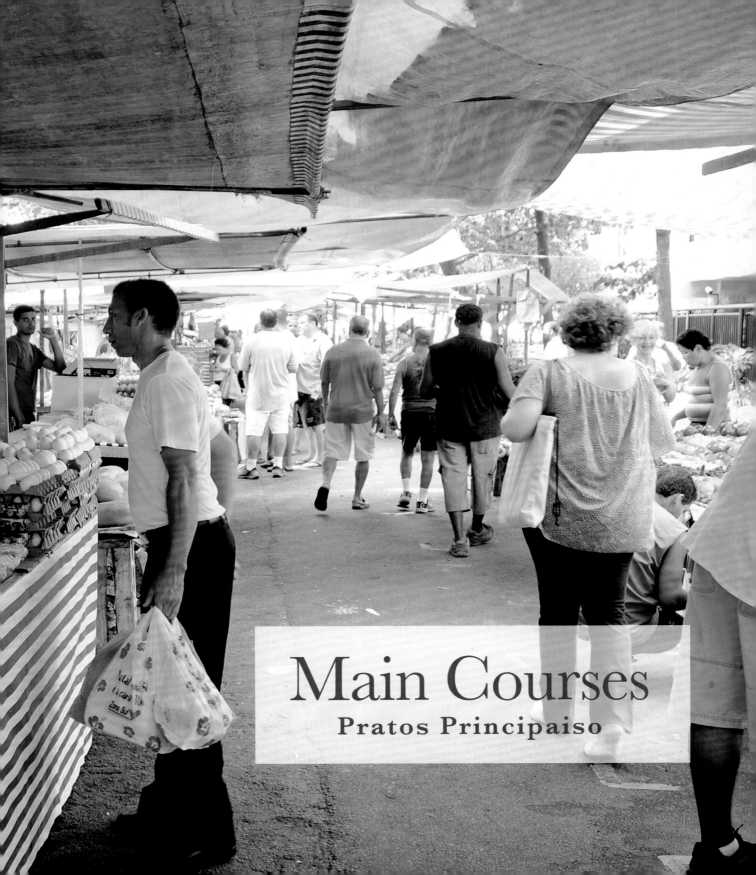

Main Courses
Pratos Principaiso

BRAZILIAN FISH STEW
Moqueca de Peixe

This fish stew couldn't be more Brazilian, but with the presence of wine and fish stock, it has an international appeal that is hard to resist. *Moqueca* is originally from the state of Bahia, and there are many versions: fish, prawn or crab are the most popular. Use this recipe as a guideline and experiment with different types of fish, such as halibut and tilapia. *Moqueca* is often served with *farofa* (see page 128), but feel free to use white rice as a side dish as well. With just a little bit of coconut milk, this colourful fish stew is rich only in looks and spirit – one spoonful will reveal how unbelievably light it is.

550g (1lb 4 oz) fish fillets, such as cod, haddock, halibut or tilapia, cut into 5-cm (2-inch) chunks

1 spring onion (white and green parts), chopped

1 small onion, chopped

1 small piece of fresh root ginger, peeled and finely chopped

4 large garlic cloves, finely chopped

5 tablespoons (palm) *dendê* oil (see Glossary)

2 tablespoons extra virgin olive oil

4 tablespoons freshly chopped coriander

⅔ green pepper, chopped

⅔ yellow pepper, chopped

350ml (12fl oz) fish stock

225ml (8fl oz) coconut milk

2 tablespoons tomato paste

1 tablespoon freshly squeezed lemon juice

sea salt and freshly ground black pepper

85g (3 oz) canned hearts of palm, drained

2 plum tomatoes, peeled, deseeded and diced

1 Prepare the marinade for the fish: in a bowl, mix together half of the spring onion, half of the onion, half of the ginger and half of the garlic. Add 2 tablespoons of the *dendê* oil, all of the olive oil and half of the coriander. Place the fish chunks in a zip-lock plastic bag and add the marinade. Rub it around the fish so that it is well distributed. Remove all the air from the plastic bag and seal it well. Place the fish in the refrigerator, covered by the marinade, and leave for at least 3 hours.

2 Take the fish out of the refrigerator 30 minutes before using. Preheat the oven to 180°C/350°F/Gas Mark 4.

3 Place the remaining 3 tablespoons of dendê oil in a large sauté pan over a medium heat. Add the remaining spring onion, onion and the green and yellow peppers and cook for about 3 minutes until they are soft.

4 Add the remaining ginger and garlic and mix well. Cook for another minute or until hot. Add the fish stock and bring to a full boil. Add the coconut milk and tomato purée, and bring to a full boil, then reduce the heat to simmer the sauce gently.

5 In the meantime, spread the fish and marinade out in a gratin dish. Pour the lemon juice on top and season lightly with salt and pepper. Bake in the oven until almost done, about 10–12 minutes.

6 Carefully transfer each chunk of fish to the pan with the sauce. Pour in any remaining juices from the fish and marinade. Braise the fish in the sauce over a low heat with the pan covered until the fish is soft and tender, about 5–8 minutes.

7 Uncover the pan, add the hearts of palm and tomatoes and heat through.

8 Taste the sauce, then season it with salt and pepper and sprinkle with the remaining coriander. Serve over rice or *farofa*.

HEARTS OF PALM

Hearts of palm, or palmito in Portuguese, are harvested from the inner core of certain palm trees such as juçara, açaí and pejibaye. Available in cans, they have a nutty, artichoke-like flavour and pair well with an endless variety of ingredients. In Brazil the most praised kind is the pupunha, from yet a fourth kind of palm tree called pupunheira, found in the Amazon. It is much larger and meatier than the ones we get in the United States. If you ever go to Brazil, make sure you try a fresh pupunha.

SALT COD WITH BACON, ONIONS, EGGS AND CRUNCHY POTATOES

Bacalhau à Brás

Cod fish is often prepared with onions and potatoes in a variety of ways. This version is a favourite of mine. Although all the ingredients are common, the result is captivating. The combination of creamy scrambled eggs with cod, the flavour bursts of bacon and onions, along with the crunch of potatoes, creates a medley new to most non-Brazilian palates. Note that when using salt cod, always allow a little planning, since you need to soak the cod for at least 24 hours, preferably for 2–3 days, in cold water in the refrigerator while changing the water at least 3 times per day. This process allows the cod to be gently poached in milk and cut into tender shreds that then mix decadently with the savoury bacon and eggs and the sweet onions.

SERVES 4–6

675g (1lb 8 oz) salt cod
600ml (1 pint) milk
2 floury potatoes, such as Desiree or Maris Piper
1 litre (1¾ pints) rapeseed oil, for deep-frying
2 rashers of bacon, finely chopped
3 tablespoons olive oil, plus extra for drizzling
2 medium onions, thinly sliced
6 large eggs, lightly beaten
3 tablespoons chopped fresh chives
sea salt and freshly ground black pepper

DRYING AND DESALTING SALT COD

The best species of cod for salting is the Atlantic cod, gadus morhua. The method of salting cod is rather simple: the fish is split in half lengthways, cleaned, deboned and separated by weight. The fish is then covered with salt and kept in plastic containers for 2–4 weeks. During this stage they lose almost all the water in their bodies, and the flesh turns from snow white to a light yellow colour. The fish is hung in designated rooms with special drying systems that maintain room temperature for another 2–4 weeks. Finally, they are sorted by weight and prepared for sale. When using salt cod, it's very important to desalt it properly: use a big plastic container, as the volume of water has to be at least 10 times bigger than the weight of the cod. I also like to use a rack or colander so that the cod is completely floating in the water.

1 Desalt the cod as per steps 1–3 on page 19.

2 Cut the potatoes into juliennes, using a mandoline. You can do this by hand, of course, but it takes longer. Let the potatoes soak in cold water as you cut them, changing the water at least once. Spread the potatoes onto a baking sheet covered with kitchen paper to air-dry for 5 minutes, but not much longer, as they will start to turn brown.

3 Pour the rapeseed oil into a heavy-based saucepan and heat to 180°C/350°F as measured by a deep-fat thermometer. If you don't have a thermometer, drop one potato into the oil – when you hear a sizzling sound and see it turning golden brown, the oil is ready. Fry the potatoes in batches until they are lightly golden brown. Carefully transfer to a plate lined with a double layer of kitchen paper and sprinkle them with table salt. You can prepare the potatoes up to a day in advance; just be sure to keep them in an airtight plastic container.

4 In a large frying pan, cook the bacon over a medium heat until lightly crisp. Turn the heat to low, add the olive oil and onions and continue to cook, stirring occasionally, until they are soft and translucent, about 10–15 minutes.

5 Add the shredded cod, then add the eggs all at once to the pan. Mix with a wooden spoon and be careful not to let the eggs dry out. You want them nice and creamy. Add a handful of the string potatoes – they will get mushy when mixed in and that's fine. Season lightly.

6 Pour everything onto a big platter, sprinkle with the chives, drizzle with olive oil and garnish with another handful of string potatoes on top.

COD WITH BABY POTATOES AND ONIONS

Bacalhau à Gomes Sá

This comforting dish is usually made with salt cod and starchy baking potatoes. I chose to use fresh cod and small, finger-shaped potatoes, creating a more delicate flavour. Olives, eggs, and fresh herbs help to complete the meal. It's easy to prepare. If you prepare this dish for more than 4 people, do not increase the amount of potatoes – too many will absorb the onion juices, drying out the dish.

SERVES 4

350g (12 oz) small potatoes, such as Charlotte, peeled
5 tablespoons extra virgin olive oil
2 large onions, thinly sliced
sea salt and freshly ground black pepper
2 large eggs, hard-boiled and thinly sliced
55g (2 oz) Kalamata olives, halved
450g (1lb) cod fillets
whole fresh chives, to garnish

1   Place the potatoes whole in a large, heavy-based saucepan. Cover them with cold water by at least 2.5cm (1 inch), add a large pinch of salt and bring to the boil. Reduce the heat to medium and simmer until the potatoes are fork-tender, about 12–15 minutes.

2   Drain the potatoes in a colander and spread them out on a plate. When they are cool enough to handle, slice the potatoes into 5-mm (¼-inch) thick slices. Set aside.

3   Pour 2 tablespoons of the olive oil into a large frying pan, add the onions and cook over low heat, stirring occasionally, until sweet and translucent, about 10–15 minutes. Resist the temptation to turn the heat to high, otherwise the onion will brown. The slower you cook the onion, the sweeter it becomes. Transfer to a large bowl.

4   Preheat the oven to 180°C/350°F/Gas Mark 4 and lightly coat a large shallow baking dish (glass or ceramic) with cooking oil spray.

5   Add the sliced potatoes to the onion and toss. Season with salt and pepper. Spread them into the prepared baking dish. Arrange the egg slices and olives on top. Drizzle over another 2 tablespoons of the olive oil.

6   Season the cod with salt and pepper and place it on top of the potato, onion, egg and olive mixture. Drizzle the remaining tablespoon olive oil on top of the fish and bake it in the oven until the fish is just cooked, about 12–15 minutes. The flesh will turn from translucent to opaque white.

7   Remove the baking dish from the oven and garnish with whole chives. Spoon the cod onto warm plates and serve hot.

MUSSELS IN COCONUT CREAM SAUCE

Mexilhões com Molho de Côco

Mussels are relatively cheap, easy to prepare, extremely tasty and go well with so many flavours. This recipe is just as much about the broth as it is about the mussel. While cooking, the mussels become tender and sweet, and exude their own juices – infusing the sauce with the perfect ocean flavour. It's worth having a piece of bread on the side to catch any leftover sauce. Choose mussels that smell like the ocean, and with tightly shut shells or shells that shut when tapped, as a sign that they are alive. Discard any mussels that don't open while cooking. Try to buy the mussels the day that you'll eat them.

SERVES 4

1.6–1.8kg (3lb 8 oz–4lb) mussels
2 tablespoons *dendê* (palm) oil (see Glossary on page 170)
½ small onion, finely chopped
about ⅓ yellow pepper, finely chopped
about ⅓ red pepper, finely chopped
about ⅓ green pepper, finely chopped
3 garlic cloves, finely chopped
225ml (8fl oz) dry white wine
400ml (14fl oz) coconut milk
sea salt and freshly ground black pepper
1 plum tomato, peeled, deseeded and diced
2 tablespoons chopped fresh coriander

1 Rinse and scrub the mussels thoroughly. Discard any mussels with cracked shells and pull off the beards.

2 In a large saucepan (big enough to handle all the mussels), warm the *dendê* oil over a medium heat. Add the onion and peppers and cook, stirring occasionally, until soft, about 3 minutes. Add the garlic and cook for another minute.

3 Add the mussels and wine. Cover the pan and cook until the mussels open their shells, shaking the pan occasionally, about 5–8 minutes (be sure not to cook any longer, or the mussels will taste rubbery).

4 Using tongs or a slotted spoon, remove the mussels and place them in a bowl. Cover with a tight-fitting lid to keep moist.

5 Bring the remaining sauce to the boil and add the coconut milk. Cook until the sauce reduces and thickens, about 5 minutes. Taste the sauce and season with salt and pepper.

6 Return the mussels and any accumulated juices in the bowl to the pan. Add the tomato, cover and cook for 2 minutes, just to reheat.

7 Divide the mussels between individual plates, spoon the sauce over them and garnish with coriander.

PRAWN STEW IN YUCCA AND COCONUT SAUCE

Bobó de Camarão

Prawns, *dendê* oil, coconut milk and peppers makes this recipe one of my favourite flavour combinations of our cuisine. It's all robed in a delicious sauce that relies on a staple vegetable in Brazil: yucca. Most Brazilians cook yucca with coconut milk, then blend it in a food processor or blender. Yucca, however, does not blend well. If you have ever tried mashing potatoes in a food processor, you know the disaster I am referring to. To solve this problem, I injected some French technique. Using white wine, prawn stock and mashed yucca (see page 32) instead of blended yucca results in a stew with better texture and taste. This is a great dish for entertaining or for a fun family meal. Serve it with *farofa* (see page 128) or white rice.

1 small yucca, about 300g (11 oz)

3 tablespoons *dendê* (palm) oil (see Glossary on page 170)

1 small onion, chopped

½ green pepper, chopped

½ yellow pepper, chopped

2 spring onions (white and green parts), chopped

2 celery sticks

4 garlic cloves, finely chopped

125ml (4fl oz) white wine

475ml (17fl oz) prawn stock (see opposite)

225ml (8fl oz) coconut milk

2 tablespoons tomato purée

450g (1lb) uncooked prawns, peeled and deveined

sea salt and freshly ground black pepper

25g (1 oz) unsalted butter

pinch of ground nutmeg

3 plum tomatoes, peeled, deseeded and diced

3 tablespoons chopped fresh coriander

1 Follow the instructions on page 32 for preparing and mashing the yucca.

2 Place the *dendê* oil, onion, peppers, spring onions and celery in a large sauté pan and cook, stirring occasionally, until they are soft and translucent, about 3 minutes.

3 Add the garlic and stir until hot. Add the white wine and reduce by half, about 1–2 minutes. Add the prawn stock and coconut milk, then bring the mixture to the boil.

4 Reduce the heat to low and add 85g (4 oz) of the mashed yucca and the tomato purée and use a whisk to help dissolve them both into the sauce. The sauce will start to thicken naturally; add up to another 85g (4 oz) of the mashed yucca if necessary. Set aside.

5 Season the prawns with salt and pepper on both sides.

6 In a medium frying pan, melt the butter over a medium heat. Add the prawns and cook until they just start to turn pink, about 1 minute each side.

7 Transfer the prawns to the saucepan. Pour in any prawn juices that remain in the frying pan and cook the prawn stew over a very low heat, covered, for 5 minutes. Taste the stew and adjust the seasoning with salt, pepper and the nutmeg. Garnish with the tomatoes and coriander.

BUYING PRAWNS

When it comes to prawns, Brazil is blessed with many varieties, all large by British standards. You can buy the larger tiger prawns uncooked and either fresh or frozen. Because every part of the prawn is packed with flavour, look for shell-on prawns and save the shells to make stock. Making fish stock from scratch is not much fun – you have to gut the fish and remove the gills and eyeballs. So I use prawn stock for all my fish and shellfish recipes and it works wonderfully while being worlds easier to prepare. See page 112 for a recipe.

PRAWNS WITH HEARTS OF PALM AND TOMATOES

Camarão com Palmito e Tomate

In this recipe, prawns are paired with hearts of palm, an ingredient that is highly entrenched in the Brazilian vernacular and easy to find fresh all over the country. In the UK, it is available tinned, carrying a mild flavour and a trace of acidity from the preserving liquids. A virtue of prawns is that they cook in a jiffy, so the key to keeping them moist is by adding them only in the final minutes of cooking. Whenever I eat shellfish, I like a touch of butter, but other than that, this dish is pretty healthy. If you would like to make it more filling, serve it with a side of white rice.

SERVES 4

475ml (17fl oz) prawn stock (see page 112)
675g (1lb 8 oz) large uncooked prawns, peeled and deveined
sea salt and freshly ground black pepper
55g (2 oz) unsalted butter
½ onion, chopped
2 spring onions, thinly sliced on the diagonal
2 garlic cloves, finely chopped
125ml (4fl oz) dry white wine
250g (9 oz) drained canned hearts of palm, cut into ½-inch rounds on the diagonal
2 plum tomatoes, peeled, deseeded and chopped
4 tablespoons chopped fresh coriander

1 Place the prawn stock in a small saucepan and keep it hot at a low simmer. Season the prawns with salt and pepper.

2 In a large frying pan, melt half of the butter. Add the prawns and cook until they turn pink and opaque, about 1 minute on each side. Immediately pour the prawns and their juices into a bowl and cover with foil.

3 Meanwhile, melt 15g (½ oz) of the butter in the same pan and add the onion and spring onions. Cook, scraping up all the brown bits left from the prawns and stirring occasionally, until soft, about 3 minutes. Add the garlic and heat. Add the white wine and reduce by half, about 2 minutes.

4 Add the prawn stock and bring to the boil, cooking until it starts to thicken, about 5 minutes. Check the seasoning and adjust if necessary. Add the hearts of palm and tomatoes and cook until hot, about 2 minutes.

5 Add the prawns and any juices that have accumulated in the bowl. Cook for 2–3 minutes just to reheat them. Add the remaining butter, adjust the seasoning if necessary and garnish with the fresh coriander.

PRAWNS WITH CHAYOTE
Camarão com Chuchu

Chayote is a mild-flavoured, light green vegetable that has been shining for a long time as one of the most basic vegetables in Brazilian home cooking. In Portuguese, it's called *chuchu*, and it grows abundantly just about anywhere it is planted. This classic dish is delicate and serene, yet bursts with extraordinary flavours mingling from the prawns and the ultra-succulent texture of the chayote. In my opinion, it needs nothing else, but if you want to add a handful of cherry tomatoes, more for colour than for taste, go ahead.

SERVES 4

350ml (12fl oz) prawn stock (see page 112)
450g (1lb) large uncooked prawns, peeled and deveined
sea salt and freshly ground black pepper
3 chayotes, about 240g (8½ oz) each
55g (2 oz) unsalted butter
½ onion, finely chopped
2 garlic cloves, finely chopped
a few drops of freshly squeezed lemon juice
4 tablespoons chopped fresh chives

1 Place the prawn stock in a small saucepan and keep at a low simmer. Season the prawns with salt and pepper on both sides.

2 Wearing rubber gloves (as chayote is very oily), cut the ends off each chayote and peel the outer skin with a vegetable peeler. Cut the chayote in half vertically from the long side and remove the core using a melon baller or a paring knife. Cut each half into 1-cm (½-inch) thick slices, then cut each slice into medium pieces on the diagonal. Place in a bowl, season with salt and pepper and toss.

3 In a saucepan, melt 25g (1 oz) of the butter over a low heat. Add the chayote and cook, stirring occasionally, without letting it turn brown, for about 3 minutes. Add the onion and continue to cook, stirring occasionally, until softened, another 3 minutes. Add the garlic and cook for another minute. Add the stock and simmer everything over a low heat until the chayote is soft and tender, about 3–5 minutes. Don't let the liquid evaporate too much.

4 In a 30-cm (12-inch) frying pan, melt the remaining butter, add the prawns to the pan and cook until they just start to turn pink and opaque, about 1 minute per side.

5 Transfer the prawns and any accumulated juices to the saucepan and simmer everything together over a low heat until the flavours start to mingle, about 2–3 minutes. Be sure not to overcook the prawns or they will taste rubbery.

6 Add the lemon juice, season with salt and pepper and garnish with the chives.

SOLE WITH COCONUT GINGER SAUCE

Linguado e Pimentões com Molho de Côco e Gengibre

Here is a simple and healthy recipe, perfect for a week-night dinner. Although fish with vegetables is often a dish you'll eat only because it's good for you, this recipe is so tasty, you might end up craving more. The coconut milk acts not only as an exciting flavour but as a thickening agent, giving body to a creamy sauce, while the ginger adds a sharp pungency that complements the texture of the fish and the sweetness of the peppers. Try to dice the peppers evenly and very small for a nicer presentation. Both the sauce and the vegetables can be prepared ahead of time. Make sure you buy coconut milk, not coconut juice (the water inside the coconut) or cream of coconut (coconut milk loaded with sugars and emulsifiers).

3 tablespoons olive oil

about ⅔ red pepper, chopped

about ⅔ yellow pepper, chopped

about ⅔ green pepper, chopped

4 shallots, finely chopped, 3 shallots, finely chopped

2 garlic cloves, finely chopped, plus 2 cloves, chopped

sea salt and freshly ground black pepper

1 tablespoon chopped fresh thyme, plus extra thyme
   sprigs to garnish

40g (1½ oz) chopped fresh ginger root

50ml (2fl oz) dry white wine

350ml (12fl oz) fish stock

225ml (8fl oz) coconut milk

4 skinless sole fillets, about 175g (6 oz) each

140g (5 oz) plain flour, for dredging

25g (1 oz) unsalted butter

1 Heat 2 tablespoons of the olive oil in a large
   sauté pan over a medium heat. Add the peppers
   and 4 shallots and cook, stirring frequently,
   until soft, about 3–5 minutes. Add the finely
   chopped garlic and cook for another minute.
   Season with salt and pepper and add the
   chopped thyme. Keep warm but off the heat.

2 To make the sauce, place the remaining olive
   oil and shallots in a medium saucepan and
   cook over a medium heat, stirring often, until
   soft and translucent, about 5 minutes. Add
   the ginger and remaining garlic and cook,
   stirring, for another 2 minutes. Pour in the
   white wine and reduce by 80 per cent.

3 Add the coconut milk, stir well and cook over
   a low heat until the sauce reaches a proper
   consistency. To test, place one tablespoon
   of sauce on a plate; it should just hold its
   shape. If the sauce is too runny, reduce a
   little longer, and if it's too thick, add a little

more coconut milk or wine. Pass the sauce
through a fine sieve into another saucepan.
Discard the solids. Season with salt and
pepper and keep warm.

4 Meanwhile, prepare the sole. Lay the fillets
   on a baking sheet and gently pat them dry
   with kitchen paper. Season with salt and
   pepper on both sides. Dredge the fish in
   flour on both sides and shake off the excess.

5 In a large frying pan, melt the butter over a
   medium heat and swirl it to cover the whole
   pan. Gently lay the fish in the pan; they
   should sizzle lightly. Try not to move the fish
   around so that it creates a golden crust on
   each side. Cook until the fillets are golden
   brown on both sides, about 2–3 minutes per
   side. Be careful when turning the fish over;
   use a fish slice to avoid cracking the crust.
   Transfer the fish to warm plates or a platter.

6 Using an offset spatula, spread a thin layer
   of the warm peppers on top of the fish.
   Spoon the sauce around the fish and garnish
   with a sprig of thyme on top.

CHOOSING FLATFISH

Dover sole is my first choice for
this dish, with its delicate flavour
and light texture. But you could use
lemon sole instead – which is not a
'true' sole but a type of plaice. My
last choice would be flounder, brill
or dab, which are less tasty, but the
flavour and body of the coconut-
ginger sauce more than makes up
for that. You could also use turbot
or tilapia.

FISH PURÉE WITH COCONUT MILK

Vatapá

Vatapá is a classic dish from Brazil's Bahia region. It is a purée of fish, bread, coconut milk, prawn stock, cashews, peanuts, onions, tomatoes, *dendê* oil, ginger and dried shrimp. The dried shrimp found outside Brazil carries more shell than meat and by the time it's ground it becomes very gritty. So I make a version without it and it is just as delicious. In Brazil, *vatapá* is mostly used as a spread or a filling for *acarajé* (I use it as a dip on page 30). Here, I use it as a bed for fresh prawns, but you can also spread it over flatbread and top it with prawns and tomatoes (see page 28). *Vatapá* can be prepared with any other white fish such as sea bass, red snapper or pollack instead of halibut. Also try a shrimp-based *vatapá*.

SERVES 6–8

75g (2¾ oz) unsalted roasted peanuts
75g (2¾ oz) unsalted roasted cashew nuts
450ml (16fl oz) prawn stock
450g (1lb) halibut
sea salt and freshly ground pepper
4 tablespoons tomato purée
2 slices white bread with crusts removed, diced
400ml (14fl oz) coconut milk
3 tablespoons *dendê* (palm) oil
½ medium onion, diced
1 spring onion (white and green parts), chopped
3 garlic cloves, finely chopped
1 teaspoon peeled and finely grated fresh root ginger, or ¼ teaspoon ground ginger
4 plum tomatoes, peeled, deseeded and diced
1 tablespoon freshly squeezed lemon juice
⅛ teaspoon turmeric
⅛ teaspoon smoked Spanish paprika

675g (1lb 8 oz) uncooked prawns, peeled and deveined
2 tablespoons *dendê* (palm) oil
a handful of chopped fresh coriander, to garnish

---

1 In the bowl of a food processor, process the peanuts and cashew nuts until they are finely ground but not quite a paste. Transfer to a bowl and set aside.

2 Bring the prawn stock to a simmer and keep over a low heat. Season the fish with salt and pepper on both sides. Carefully immerse the fish in the simmering stock and poach until cooked through, about 3–5 minutes. Do not let the liquid boil. Transfer the fish to a plate and cover with foil.

3 Add the tomato purée to the stock and whisk until completely dissolved. Turn off the heat.

4 In a medium bowl, soak the bread in the coconut milk until it becomes moist and soft, about 5 minutes. Set aside.

5 Pour the *dendê* oil into a large saucepan, add the onion and spring onion and cook over a medium heat, stirring occasionally, until soft, about 3–4 minutes. Add the garlic and ginger and cook for another minute.

6 Place the fish in the bowl of a food processor. Add the bread with all of the coconut milk. Process until you have a coarse fish purée, about 2 minutes. Carefully pour the fish purée into the saucepan, scraping the side of the bowl with a spatula to get it all out.

7 Add the ground nuts and tomatoes and stir everything well with a wooden spoon. Add the prawn stock, lemon juice, turmeric and

paprika and season with salt and pepper. Simmer for 5–10 minutes, partially covered. Keep warm, or store the *vatapá* in an airtight plastic container for up to 2 days in the refrigerator.

8 Season the prawns with salt and pepper on both sides.

9 Pour the *dendê* oil into a large frying pan over a medium heat. Add the prawns and cook until they just turn pink, about 30 seconds–1 minute on each side.

10 To serve, place a spoonful of *vatapá* on a bowl and top with prawns. Pour any of the *dendê* oil remaining in the pan over the prawns. Garnish with the fresh coriander.

FISH IN SPICED HONEY

Filet de Peixe ao Mel Picante

My friends Patty and Sergey Boyce are beekeepers in Connecticut, and I learnt from them that honey can absorb a wide variety of flavours when infused with certain ingredients. After a lesson on cooking with honey and a freshly harvested golden jar in my hands, I was inspired. After a few hours of marinating, you'll be rewarded with a sweet-crusted fish that is full of flavour but with a delicate, snow white inside (you could try this with chicken, too). Make sure to save some spiced honey to baste the fish while cooking, but do it at the end of the cooking process, otherwise the honey might caramelise and harden in the pan.

SERVES 4

175ml (6fl oz) sherry vinegar
85g (3 oz) honey
1 tablespoon soy sauce
2 tablespoons freshly squeezed orange juice
1 cinnamon stick
½ teaspoon fennel seeds
4 cardamom pods
25g (1 oz) fresh root ginger, peeled and finely chopped

4 centre-cut, skinless halibut fillets, 175g (6 oz) each
sea salt and freshly ground black pepper
2 tablespoons extra virgin olive oil

1 Place the first 8 ingredients in a medium saucepan and bring to the boil. Reduce the heat to low and simmer until the liquid reduces to a light syrupy consistency, about 4–6 minutes. Remove from the heat and leave to cool completely in the pan. You can refrigerate the honey reduction in an airtight plastic container for up to 5 days.

2 Place the halibut fillets in a large zip-lock plastic bag and pour all of the honey reduction (except 2–3 tablespoons) with all the spices into the bag. Rub the reduction around the fish until the fillets are evenly coated. Remove the air from the plastic bag and seal well. Place in the refrigerator for 3–5 hours.

3 Remove the fish from the refrigerator at least 20 minutes before cooking. Preheat the oven to 190°C/375°F/Gas Mark 5.

4 Remove the fish from the honey reduction and wipe off any remaining fennel seeds, but do not pat dry, as you want the sugar in the honey to glaze the fish. Season with salt and pepper.

5 Heat the olive oil in a large, ovenproof frying pan over a medium to high heat. Add the fish and cook until lightly golden brown, about 2–3 minutes per side. Pour the reserved reduction over the fish and transfer the pan to the oven. Bake until the fish is cooked through, about 5 minutes. Transfer the fish to 4 dinner plates and spoon any remaining reduction on top.

SEA BASS WITH CASHEW SOY SAUCE

Peixe com Molho de Manteiga e Castanhas

Inspired by both Asian and Brazilian cuisines, this recipe is perfect for a week-night dinner. Soy sauce makes a fine sauce here, thinned with nutty browned butter, lemon juice, shallots and a dash of sugar. But that's just the beginning. You add peanuts, cashews and chives before serving. Ultimately, you'll be rewarded with a mahogany-coloured, intensely flavoured and crunchy sauce. Feel free to use this sauce with other fish as well, such as halibut, monkfish, salmon and scallops. Just be sure to adapt the cooking time for each fish.

SERVES 4

200g (7 oz) unsalted butter
3 tablespoons freshly squeezed lemon juice
2 tablespoons soy sauce
1 shallot, finely chopped
$\frac{1}{8}$ teaspoon sugar
4 skin-on sea bass fillets, 140g (5 oz) each
sea salt and freshly ground black pepper
50g (1¾ oz) roasted cashew nuts, roughly chopped
50g (1¾ oz) roasted peanuts, roughly chopped
2 tablespoons chopped fresh chives

1 In a medium saucepan over a low heat, melt 175g (6 oz) of the butter until it develops a light golden brown colour. Be careful not to let it burn. Add the lemon juice, soy sauce, shallot and sugar. Whisk the sauce, then remove the pan from the heat, but keep it in a warm spot on the hob.

2 Make 2 or 3 small diagonal cuts on the skin of the fish without piercing the flesh. Season with salt and pepper on both sides.

3 In a large, non-stick frying pan over a medium heat, melt the remaining butter and add the fish, skin-side down. Depending on the thickness of the fish, it might curl up, so use a fish slice to press the skin down against the pan, making sure that it becomes crispy. Cook until the fish turns opaque, about 2 minutes on each side.

4 Reheat the sauce gently over a low heat and whisk vigorously to blend it smooth. Add the cashew nuts, peanuts and chives.

5 To serve, arrange the fish on 4 warm plates and spoon the sauce on top.

BAKED SHELLFISH FRITTATA

Torta Capixaba

When you see the word *capixaba*, you can be sure that whatever is being served originates from the state of Espirito Santo, located above the state of Rio de Janeiro, along Brazil's southeastern coast. Traditional *Torta Capixaba* is a giant mixture of fish and shellfish of all types in a frittata with additional whisked egg whites on top; everything is baked in an old-style clay baking dish. It certainly served as my template for this short-order frittata, which is definitely a more approachable dish than the original. Use any combination of shellfish you like and keep the quantities I've provided as your guidelines. You can use clams, lobster, mussels, squid, or oysters. This recipe should help you cook the shellfish to perfection: first, they're given a quick toss on the hob, then they are mixed with lightly beaten eggs and poured into a baking dish (you can use individual ramekins, too) and baked in the oven until the eggs are just set. As a matter of taste, eggs must not be overcooked, so be as careful when baking the frittata as you are when cooking the shellfish, and you'll have a stunning dinner at the table.

SERVES 4

2 tablespoons olive oil

1 medium onion, thinly sliced

1 spring onion, thinly sliced on the diagonal

3 cloves garlic, finely chopped

225g (8 oz) uncooked prawns, shelled

115g (4 oz) shelled uncooked scallops

sea salt and freshly ground black pepper

225g (8 oz) cooked white crabmeat

2 plum tomatoes, peeled, deseeded and thinly sliced

2 tablespoons green olives, stoned and halved (optional)

4 large eggs

2 tablespoons chopped fresh parsley

23-cm (9-inch) round baking dish

1 Preheat the oven to 180°C/350°F/Gas Mark 4. Grease the baking dish with cooking oil spray.

2 Pour the olive oil into a large sauté pan, add the onion and spring onion and cook over a medium heat, stirring occasionally, until soft, about 3 minutes. Be careful not to let them brown. Add the garlic and cook for another minute.

3 Season the prawns and scallops with sea salt on all sides. Add them to the pan, reduce the heat to low and cook until they start to turn opaque, about 2 minutes. Add the crab, tomatoes and green olives, if using, and stir everything together. Season with salt and pepper and transfer to a bowl.

4   In a separate medium bowl, break in the eggs and season with salt and pepper. Lightly whisk the eggs and pour them into the shellfish mixture. Add the parsley and fold everything together with a rubber spatula.

5   Pour the mixture into the prepared baking dish and bake in the oven until the eggs are just set, about 20–30 minutes. Do not overcook, or the eggs will dry out.

6   To serve, remove the dish from the oven and rush it to the table. Divide it between warm dinner plates and enjoy.

SALMON WITH CAIPIRINHA RISOTTO

Salmon com Risotto de Caipirinha

I like to incorporate the flavours of a Caipirinha (see page 14) into other dishes, both sweet and savoury. I always think of risotto as being a great flavour receptor, so I decided to try a caipirinha risotto. I thought of the classic Italian *penne alla vodka* where the pasta receives a boost of alcohol. This is an excellent rice dish with many kinds of fish – salmon is my favourite, but scallops, halibut, skate and prawns all work splendidly with the sharp flavours of lime and cachaça in this warm and creamy risotto. I emphasise the word creamy – all too often I find risottos are served thick, dried and pasty. Add a few tablespoons of stock just before serving to ensure a creamy state. This is a glamorous and different dish to make for an entertaining, yet not overly complicated, week-night dinner.

generous 1 litre (1¾ pints) prawn stock (see page 112)

70g (2½ oz) unsalted butter

4 tablespoons extra virgin olive oil, plus extra for drizzling

½ medium onion, finely diced

200g (7 oz) Arborio rice

4 skinless salmon fillets, 115g (4 oz) each

sea salt and freshly ground black pepper

grated zest of 1 lime

4 teaspoons freshly squeezed lime juice

75ml (2½ oz) cachaça

2 tablespoons chopped fresh dill, plus a few
  sprigs to garnish

1 tablespoon crème fraîche

1   In a large saucepan, bring the stock to the
boil over a high heat. Reduce the heat to low
and keep the stock at a slow, steady simmer.

2   Melt 2 tablespoons of the butter and
2 tablespoons of the olive oil in a large
sauté pan over a medium heat. Add the
onion and cook, stirring often, until soft and
translucent, about 5 minutes. Add the rice
and cook while still stirring until all the
grains are coated with the onion and butter
and the rice looks shiny, about 3 minutes.

3   Add one large ladle of simmering stock at a
time. Cook, stirring often, until the liquid is
absorbed by the rice. Add another ladle and
keep cooking and stirring. Continue adding
ladles of stock only when the previous has
been completely absorbed. Keep the heat
low because you'll prepare the salmon while
the risotto is cooking.

4   Season the salmon fillets on both sides with
salt and pepper.

5   In a large frying pan over a medium heat,
heat the remaining 2 tablespoons olive oil.
Add the salmon, top-side down, and cook for
about 2 minutes on each side (if you like your
salmon well done, cook it a little longer).
Try to coordinate the cooking of the salmon
with the risotto; the rice should be just a few
minutes from being done by the time the
fillets are finished.

6   The rice should be al dente and almost all
of the liquid absorbed within 15 minutes
of starting. Remove it from the heat and
season with salt and pepper. Add the lime
zest and juice, cachaça and chopped dill.
Mix everything well with a wooden spoon.

7   Add the remaining butter and crème fraîche.
Add another tablespoon or so of stock if the
risotto has absorbed all of its liquid.

8   Spoon the risotto into warm bowls. Place the
salmon on top and garnish with a dill sprig and
a drizzle of olive oil.

RISOTTO COOKING TIP

You've probably heard this many times
before, but when making risotto, try to
keep a slight crunchiness to the grain,
cooking it al dente. Risotto can be
prepared ahead of time, despite what
some may tell you: remove it from the
hob after the second or third addition
of liquid and spread it onto a baking
tray to cool it down. Resume the
cooking when you are ready to cook
the fish.

TILAPIA WITH AÇAÍ SAUCE

Peixe no Molho de Açaí

15g (½ oz) unsalted butter
1 medium shallot, finely chopped
1 bay leaf
85g (3 oz) frozen açai pulp, thawed
75ml (2½fl oz) crème de cassis
2 tablespoons raspberry jam
125ml (4fl oz) prawn stock (see page 112)
sea salt and freshly ground black pepper
50ml (2fl oz) double cream

4 skinless tilapia fillets, 175g (6 oz) each
70g (2½ oz) plain flour
2 tablespoons olive oil
3 tablespoons chopped mint leaves, to garnish

1   Melt the butter in a medium saucepan over a medium heat. Add the shallot and cook, stirring frequently, until soft, about 2–3 minutes.

2   Add the bay leaf, açai, cassis, raspberry jam and prawn stock. Bring everything to the boil, then reduce the heat to low and cook at a quiet simmer until the sauce starts to become thick and syrupy, about 10 minutes. Season lightly with salt and pepper.

3   Strain the sauce through a fine sieve into a small saucepan. Add the double cream and bring to a simmer again until blended, about 2 minutes. The sauce can be refrigerated in an airtight container for up to 2 days.

Açai, the little crown jewel berry from the Amazon, is taking America by storm due to its high nutritional content. It can be a truly interesting ingredient if bought in frozen pulps, and can be prepared in many ways, both sweet or savoury, just like a berry. Its taste is so strong – a blend of red wine and chocolate – that the fruit is often matched with other berries to lighten it up a little. In this recipe, *açai* adds a depth of flavour to a sauce that complements a simply cooked fish. Monkfish, halibut or even swordfish all work well with the sweet taste of *açai*, but the humble tilapia, lightly crisped in flour and olive oil, is my favourite.

4   Season the fish on both sides with salt and pepper. Dredge the fish in the flour on both sides and shake off the excess.

5   Pour the olive oil into a large, non-stick frying pan and cook the fish over a medium heat until it's lightly golden brown, about 2–3 minutes per side. Transfer the fish to a plate lined with kitchen paper to absorb the excess oil.

6   Serve the fish on a warm plate and spoon the sauce on top and around. Garnish with the mint.

CHICKEN FEIJOADA

Feijoada de Galinha

The national dish of Brazil, *feijoada* is a crowd pleaser. This recipe is a faster version, but it certainly retains all the warmth of the slow-simmered original. I developed this recipe with a large party in mind, but I have also been using it for week-night dinners by simply using one chicken and halving the amount of beans. My favourite way to vary this recipe is to use different types of beans. I encourage you to follow suit, but be advised that different types, and indeed different brands of beans, will vary the cooking time substantially. Different bean varieties (as long as they are dried beans) like pinto, red kidney and haricot all blend splendidly in this *feijoada*. While you can't get too fancy with a *feijoada*, you also can't get closer to our cuisine's roots. And if you crave the taste of Brazil like I do, eat it again the next day because it reheats fantastically. Serve with white rice or *farofa* (see page 128).

SERVES 8–10

450g (1lb) black beans, picked over and rinsed

2 whole chickens, 1.6–1.8kg (3½–4lb), cut into
   6 pieces each, with the skin on

sea salt and freshly ground black pepper

4 tablespoons rapeseed oil

125ml (4fl oz) white wine

1 onion, chopped

2 celery sticks, finely chopped

4 spring onions (green and white parts), finely chopped

1 green pepper, finely chopped

5 garlic cloves, finely chopped

3 bay leaves

freshly grated nutmeg

cayenne pepper

2 tablespoons chopped fresh parsley

1   Place the beans in a very large saucepan, and cover them with cold water by 5cm (2 inches). Cover the pan and bring the water to the boil over a high heat. Reduce the heat to medium-high and cook the beans, covered, until they are just cooked but not too mushy, about 1–1½ hours. At this point the liquid will still look thin and clear. Keep the beans in the liquid and set them aside. This step can be completed up to 2 days ahead of time; just keep the beans and the liquid in an airtight plastic container in the refrigerator.

2   While the beans are cooking, prepare the chicken and vegetables. Pat the chicken pieces dry with kitchen paper and season with salt and pepper on both sides.

3   Pour 2 tablespoons of the rapeseed oil into a large sauté pan and cook the chicken, in batches, over a medium heat until it is golden brown, about 4 minutes per side. Transfer to a bowl and cover with foil, making sure that the steam cannot escape.

4   Use the white wine to deglaze the pan by scraping the pan with a wooden spoon, making sure all the brown bits and juices are transferred to the liquid. Boil until the liquid is well infused with flavour, then strain it into a bowl. Set aside.

5   Pour the remaining 2 tablespoons oil into a large, flameproof casserole and cook the onion, celery, spring onions and pepper over a medium heat, stirring, until soft, about 3 minutes. Add the garlic and cook for another minute. Add the chicken and all the juices that may have accumulated in the bowl. Add the reserved beans and all their liquid, and the strained deglazing liquid. The chicken should be covered almost entirely with the beans, vegetables and liquid.

6   Add the bay leaves and simmer over a very low heat with the pan uncovered so that the liquid has a chance to reduce and thicken. Cook until the chicken meat is tender and sliding off the bone, about 1–1½ hours.

7   Before finishing, slightly tilt the pan and scoop out any chicken fat. The black bean sauce should be glossy and earthy. Season to taste with salt, pepper, nutmeg and cayenne. Top with the chopped parsley.

8   To serve, place a piece of chicken in a bowl over the starch of your choice, and top with a ladle of the bean sauce.

CHICKEN AND PLANTAIN MOQUECA

Moqueca de Galinha e Banana-da-Terra

This is a tame version of the traditional seafood *moqueca*. The plantain brings a soft sweetness and plenty of starch to the stew. Some recipes call for green plantains, which are treated like a potato, but true Brazilians prefer to eat their plantains ripe or semi-ripe, when the fruit has a fuller balance of sweetness and starch, and carries more juice. This is a straightforward braising dish that takes a bit longer than the fish version (about 1½ hours), but when you taste the dynamic combination of chicken and plantains, you will experience comforting flavours and textures that make this *moqueca* worth the wait.

SERVES 4–6

1 whole chicken, about 1.6kg (3½lb), cut into 8 pieces with the skin on

sea salt and freshly ground black pepper

4 tablespoons *dendê* (palm) oil (see Glossary on page 170)

1 medium onion, thinly sliced

2 spring onions, sliced on the diagonal

½ green pepper, thinly sliced

125ml (4fl oz) white wine

4 garlic cloves, finely chopped

1 small piece of fresh root ginger, peeled and finely grated

700ml (1¼ pints) chicken stock

350ml (12fl oz) coconut milk

3 tablespoons tomato purée

2 bay leaves

450g (1lb) ripe plantains (look for yellow and black-speckled skin)

3 plum tomatoes, peeled, deseeded and sliced

4 tablespoons chopped fresh coriander

1 Place the chicken pieces in a medium bowl. Season with salt, pepper and 2 tablespoons of the *dendê* oil. Rub the chicken all over with the oil, making sure that it is well distributed. Cover the bowl with clingfilm and leave to marinate at room temperature for 15–30 minutes.

2 Pour the remaining oil into a large flameproof casserole and swirl around so that the entire base is covered. Add the chicken pieces, skin-side down, and brown them lightly over a medium heat for 3 minutes per side.

3   Using a pair of tongs, transfer the chicken pieces to a clean bowl and cover with foil, making sure that no steam can escape.

4   Add the onion, spring onions and pepper to the pan and cook them in the left-over oil, stirring often, until they become soft, about 4 minutes. Add the white wine and reduce by half, while using a wooden spoon to scrape the brown bits that remain in the pan. Add the garlic and ginger and cook, stirring, for another minute. Add the chicken stock, coconut milk, tomato purée and bay leaves and bring to the boil.

5   Reduce the heat to the lowest setting. Add the chicken and any remaining juices that have accumulated in the bowl. Season lightly with salt and pepper. Simmer, covered, until the chicken starts to become tender, about 1 hour.

6   Meanwhile, trim the ends off the plantains and cut 3–4 vertical slits in the skin, making sure not to cut deep into the fruit. Peel and cut the plantains into 2.5-cm (1-inch) chunks.

7   Add the plantains to the *moqueca* after it has been simmering for an hour. Cover and continue to simmer until the plantains become soft but not mushy, about 10–15 minutes. If the liquid seems too runny, uncover the pan and continue to simmer, allowing the steam to evaporate and thicken the stew. Season with salt and pepper.

8   Just a few minutes before serving, add the tomatoes. Garnish with the fresh coriander and serve over white rice or *farofa* (see page 128).

BRAZILIAN CHICKEN EMPANADA

Empadão de Frango

This is a delicious savoury tart of shredded chicken encased in a buttery and flaky crust. With the addition of sweetcorn, peas, tomatoes and hearts of palm, it is a great meal in itself with a green salad on the side. This recipe yields two tarts from just one chicken. Once assembled, the tarts can be stored unbaked in the refrigerator (covered loosely with clingfilm) for up to 3 days or frozen for up to a month. It's easy to add other vegetables or types of meat to the filling. Shredded duck or turkey make excellent variations.

1 For the pastry, place the flour and salt in a bowl and set aside. In the bowl of an electric mixer fitted with the paddle attachment, beat the butter at medium speed until creamy. Add the eggs and milk. Add the flour and salt and turn the speed to low. Depending on the humidity, you may need up to 3 tablespoons water to help the dough form into a ball.

2 Place the ball of dough onto a floured surface and press into a flat disc. Wrap in clingfilm and refrigerate for at least 30 minutes.

3 Meanwhile, prepare the filling. In a medium saucepan, bring the stock to the boil over a high heat. Reduce the heat to low and add the tomato purée, whisking well to dissolve.

SERVES 4–6

FOR THE PASTRY

450g (1lb) plain flour, sifted, plus extra for dusting
4 teaspoons salt
350g (12 oz) unsalted butter, chilled
2 eggs
60ml (2fl oz) full-fat milk

FOR THE FILLING

1.2 litres (2 pints) chicken stock (see page 112)
2 tablespoons tomato purée
115g (4 oz) unsalted butter
140g (5 oz) plain flour
sea salt and freshly ground black pepper
freshly grated nutmeg
2 tablespoons extra virgin olive oil
1 large onion, chopped
6 garlic cloves, finely chopped
140g (5 oz) frozen peas, thawed
140g (5 oz) frozen sweetcorn kernels, thawed
175g (6 oz) tinned, drained hearts of palm, diced
3 plum tomatoes, peeled, deseeded and diced
675g (1lb 8 oz) shredded cooked chicken, (light and
   dark meat from one 2kg (4lb 8 oz) cooked chicken)
25g (1 oz) chopped fresh chives

1 beaten egg, for glazing
2 x 2-cm (8-inch) round ceramic flan dishes

4   Melt the butter in a different saucepan over a low heat. Add the flour all at once and stir to make a roux, about 2 minutes. Add the stock and whisk constantly over a medium heat, until it thickens. Season with salt, pepper and nutmeg and set aside.

5   Warm the olive oil in a large saucepan over a low heat. Add the onion and cook, stirring occasionally, until soft and translucent, about 2 minutes. Add the garlic and cook for another minute. Add the peas, sweetcorn, hearts of palm and tomatoes, stirring constantly. Add the chicken and cook for 5 minutes. Season with salt, pepper and nutmeg. Transfer to a large bowl.

6   Pour the creamy chicken stock into the bowl and mix well. Add the chives and adjust the seasoning. Spread the filling onto a baking tray and let cool completely before assembling. Remove the dough from the refrigerator at least 20 minutes before rolling.

7   Cut the dough into 4 pieces. On a lightly floured surface, roll one piece of dough into a round about 2mm (1/16 inch) thick. Unroll the dough onto one flan dish and up to the side, leaving some extra dough hanging over the edge. Spread half of the filling inside the pastry case. Using a pastry brush dipped in water, lightly moisten the edges of the bottom crust.

8   Repeat the rolling process with another round of dough and centre it over the chicken filling. Fold a bit of extra top dough onto the flan dish. Press the top crust against the bottom crust in an attractive way with your fingers, then trim the overhang from both crusts. Using a paring knife, cut an X in the centre of the crust to vent while baking.

9   Repeat steps 7–8 for the second pie. Place the empadão in the refrigerator for at least

1 hour before baking. At this point you can cover them with clingfilm and store in the refrigerator for up to 3 days or freeze for up to 3 months.

10 Preheat oven to 180°C/350°F/Gas Mark 4. Place an empadão on a baking sheet and bake on the centre rack of the oven until the top looks lightly brown, about 30–40 minutes.

11 Remove from the oven, brush the top crust with the beaten egg and return to the oven until the crust is golden brown, about 10–15 minutes.

12 Transfer the empadão to a rack and let it rest for 20 minutes before serving. Unlike a traditional chicken pie, which is served bubbling out of the oven, the empadão (or other sizes of empada) should never be served too hot. To best enjoy it, serve it warm.

CHICKEN, PRAWN, PEANUT AND CASHEW STEW

Xim-Xim de Galinha

This stew is about simple ingredients with an exotic result. The favourite Bahian combination of chicken and prawns comes together in a creamy sauce. The nuts serve as the perfect binding agents for the coconut milk and chicken stock, but they have to be finely ground – if they are too coarse, they just won't do the work. On the other hand, you have to be careful not to turn the nuts into a paste. The recipe can be prepared up to 2 days ahead of time and reheats extremely well. If you prefer to make it ahead of time, it's best not to add the prawns to the pan until 5 minutes before serving. I like to serve this dish by itself, but if you would like a starch to go with it, white rice or *farofa* (see page 128) would be nice.

SERVES 6–8

1 whole chicken, about 1.3–1.8kg (3–4lb), cut into 8 pieces with the skin on
3 garlic cloves, roughly chopped
3 tablespoons freshly squeezed lime juice
225g (8 oz) uncooked prawns, peeled and deveined
4 tablespoons *dendê* (palm) oil
75g (2¾ oz) unsalted roasted peanuts
75g (2¾ oz) unsalted roasted cashew nuts
sea salt and freshly ground black pepper
4 tablespoons extra virgin olive oil
1 medium onion, finely chopped
2 spring onions (white and green parts), chopped
4 plum tomatoes, peeled, deseeded and diced
1 tablespoon tomato purée
350ml (12fl oz) coconut milk
350ml (12fl oz) chicken stock
¼ teaspoon turmeric
⅛ teaspoon paprika
a handful of chopped fresh coriander

1 Place the chicken pieces in a medium bowl and add the garlic and lime juice. Rub the chicken all over with the juice, making sure that it is well distributed. Cover the bowl with clingfilm and leave to marinate at room temperature for 15–30 minutes.

2 In another bowl, place the prawns and 2 tablespoons of the *dendê* oil. Cover the bowl with clingfilm and leave to marinate for 15 minutes at room temperature. (If you are making the dish ahead of time, do not marinate the prawns at this stage.)

3 Meanwhile, in the bowl of a food processor, process the cashew nuts and peanuts until they are finely ground but don't become a paste. Transfer to a bowl and set aside.

4 Remove the chicken from the marinade and wipe off any remaining garlic. Lightly pat the chicken dry with kitchen paper and season with salt and pepper on both sides.

5 Pour 2 tablespoons of the olive oil into a large sauté pan and cook the chicken pieces over a medium heat until they are lightly browned, about 3 minutes on each side. You don't want the chicken to cook completely, as it will finish during braising. If necessary, cook in batches, and as you remove the chicken pieces, place them in a bowl and cover them with foil to keep them warm.

6 Add the remaining olive oil and cook the onion and spring onions, stirring occasionally and scraping the brown bits off the bottom of the pan, until the onions are soft, about 2 minutes. Add the tomatoes, tomato purée, and ground nuts and cook, stirring to blend well, for about 1 minute. Add the coconut milk, chicken stock, turmeric and paprika and bring the sauce to a simmer.

7 Reduce the heat to its lowest setting, then add the chicken pieces and all the juices that have accumulated in the bowl. Cover and simmer until the chicken is cooked through, although it should remain tender and moist, about 25–30 minutes. (Reserve the stew at this point if you want to serve it at a later date. Store it in an airtight plastic container in the refrigerator for up to 2 days.)

8 Meanwhile, remove the prawns from the bowl and pat them dry. Season with salt and pepper on both sides.

9 In a medium frying pan, heat the remaining *dendê* oil and cook the prawns until they start to turn pink, about 1 minute per side.

10 Pour the prawns and any remaining dendê oil from the pan into the chicken stew, cover and cook so that the prawns have a chance to braise with the chicken, about 3–4 minutes. At this point the mixture should look orange and the nuts will have thickened the stew but also made it slightly gritty. You want it to be just a little pasty from the nuts. If the stew is too thick, add another tablespoon or so of chicken stock. Adjust the seasoning with salt and pepper. Garnish with the fresh coriander.

CUTTING CHICKEN

When cutting up the chicken, aim for 2 wings, 2 breasts, 2 drumsticks and 2 thighs. If that takes up a lot of space in the pan, requiring you to use 2 frying pans, you can cut the chicken into 6 pieces, leaving the thigh and drumstick attached and cutting them apart only when they reach the braising stage. You can also buy the chicken pre-cut from the supermarket or butcher's.

SLOW-ROASTED DUCK BREAST WITH CUPUAÇÚ SAUCE

Peito de Pato Assado com Molho de Cupuaçú

Duck pairs well with flavours from all over the world and cooking duck with a sweet fruit sauce is classic. I decided to experiment with fruits for a small duck breast, one that would cook quickly for a week-night dinner, and thought of cupuaçu (see Glossary on page 170) because I love its banana-like consistency and its tangy qualities fit perfectly with the outer layer of fat and the sweetness of the duck meat. Serve with a green vegetable such as spring greens (see page 123) or broccoli.

SERVES 2

2 skin-on duck breasts, 200–225g (7–8 oz) each
sea salt and freshly ground black pepper

FOR THE SAUCE
1 tablespoon olive oil
2 large shallots, roughly chopped
175ml (6fl oz) chicken stock (see page 112)
140g (5 oz) cupuaçú pulp, thawed
2 tablespoons orange marmalade
1 tablespoon honey
40g (1½ oz) unsalted butter, chilled and cubed

1 Remove the duck breasts from the refrigerator about 1 hour before cooking. Preheat the oven to 140°C/275°F/Gas Mark 1.

2 Trim the excess fat from the duck, leaving a layer on one side. Trim any silver skin and remove the small tendon from the duck breast to allow even cooking. Score the fat side with 4–5 cuts in a crosshatch pattern, being careful not to pierce the meat. Season both sides with salt and pepper – lightly on the flesh side and a little heavier on the fat.

3 Place the duck, fat-side down, in a medium ovenproof frying pan over a high heat. The pan should sizzle on contact with the duck. Cook until browned, about 2 minutes. Spoon any rendered fat into a bowl. Turn the duck over and quickly sear the flesh, about 1 minute.

4 Immediately transfer the frying pan to the oven and slow-roast the duck until the meat is cooked rare to medium rare all the way through, about 12–14 minutes.

5 Meanwhile, prepare the sauce. Pour the olive oil into a medium saucepan and cook the shallots over a medium heat until soft and translucent, about 2 minutes. Add the chicken stock, cupuaçú pulp, orange marmalade and honey and simmer over a medium to low heat until the sauce reaches a syrupy consistency, about 5 minutes.

6 Strain the sauce through a fine sieve into another saucepan. You will have about 225ml (8fl oz) cup. Discard the solids. Bring the sauce back to a simmer over a very low heat.

7 Add the cold butter and whisk it into the sauce, about 2 minutes. Once the butter is added to the sauce, don't boil it or it will curdle. Keep the heat very low and swirl the pan often. Season with salt and pepper.

8 Remove the duck from the oven and let it rest for at least 5 minutes. Slice on the diagonal and serve with some sauce spooned on top.

COOKING DUCK

Some people are afraid of cooking duck at home, especially when it comes to the breast. The meat has a tendency to become chewy if served rare, which is how we all learn duck needs to be served. Cooked correctly, though, duck breast is quite simple to prepare. The key to perfection is to sauté the breast, skin-side down, until it's nicely browned, then roast it slowly over a low temperature so that the fat has time to render and the meat is cooked equally rare as opposed to seared on the edges and red in the centre.

The three most common breeds of farmed, as opposed to wild, duck for cooking are the British Aylesbury and Gressingham, and the French Barbary. The whole birds are sold, at various heights, for roasting under six months of age, which actually means they are ducklings. Duck breasts, with or without skin and on or off the bone, are widely available in supermarkets all year round. The much smaller and gamier, wild duck – usually Mallard – is on offer only from October to December.

CHICKEN BRAISED WITH CARAMELISED ONIONS

Galinha Moreninha

Lourdes Paixão is a wonderful grandmotherly figure who cooks by memory the food of her home in Minas Gerais, where most of the cuisine is hearty and earthy. She is the kind of cook who doesn't use a chopping board – she holds vegetables with one hand and cuts them with a small knife in the other over a plastic bowl. She cooks under any circumstances, with any equipment, on any hob, and in any kitchen. One of her best dishes is this chicken dish, a cross between French onion soup and osso bucco. The onions are caramelised and the legs are slowly braised until the meat falls apart. The result is a velvety chicken stew, full of flavour.

SERVES 4–6

4 whole chicken legs, cut into legs and thighs
sea salt and freshly ground pepper
2 tablespoons olive oil
125ml (4fl oz) Madeira
2 large onions, finely sliced
3 garlic cloves, sliced
700ml (1 ¼ pints) veal stock (see page 113)
2 plum tomatoes, peeled, deseeded and chopped
2 tablespoons chopped fresh parsley

1   Season the chicken pieces with salt and pepper.

2   Heat the olive oil in a large frying pan over a medium-high heat. Add the chicken pieces, skin-side down, and cook until they are golden brown, about 4 minutes per side. Transfer to a bowl and cover with foil.

3   Turn the heat to low and add the onions. Cook, stirring frequently, until they caramelise, about 25–30 minutes. If you see the onions burning on the sides, add a tablespoon of water.

4   Add the garlic and cook for another minute. Deglaze with the Madeira and reduce almost completely. Add the veal stock and bring to the boil.

5   Return the chicken to the pan and and any juices that have accumulated in the bowl. Braise over a very low heat for 2 hours, with the pan partly covered (if the liquid is too thin, remove the lid to evaporate).

6   Add the tomatoes, season with salt and pepper to taste and sprinkle with the fresh parsley. Serve over white rice or *farofa* (see page 128).

CHICKEN BEEF ROULADE

Enrolado de Bife com Frango

SERVES 6–8

1 skirt steak, about 675g (1lb 8 oz)

freshly ground black pepper

350g (12 oz) chicken mince

2 spring onions (white and green parts), finely chopped

1 celery stick, finely chopped

½ red onion, chopped

about ⅔ yellow pepper, finely chopped

about ⅔ red pepper, finely chopped

1 small carrot, peeled and finely diced

4 garlic cloves, finely chopped

3 tablespoons chopped fresh parsley

3 tablespoons extra virgin olive oil

1 tablespoon soy sauce

1 chicken stock cube, grated into a powder

2 teaspoons sea salt, plus extra for seasoning

Eronária de Souza is from Goiás, and grew up surrounded by yucca, pequi, guaraná, turmeric and all sorts of exotic foods. When I was hunting for recipes from this region, she told me about a meat stuffed with chicken, a speciality from Goiás. At first, it seemed like an odd combination, but when I tasted it, I loved it. The roulade is slowly roasted and presents a spectrum of textures: crusty meat around the edges and moist chicken mince stuffing packed with aromatic flavours in the centre.

1 Trim the fat and silver skin from the steak. Butterfly the meat (slice in half horizontally, but keep in one piece), working across the grain. Season with salt and pepper. Set aside.

2 Place the chicken mince in a large bowl. Stir in the spring onions, celery, red onion, peppers, carrot, garlic, parsley, 1 tablespoon of the olive oil, the soy sauce and stock cube. Season with salt and pepper. Spread inside the steak, making sure to leave a 5-cm (2-inch) edge on all sides. Roll up, folding some steak over the ends to avoid the mince escaping. Tie the roulade with string, making a knot in 5–6 places. Wrap in clingfilm and refrigerate for 1–2 days.

3 Bring the roulade to room temperature at least 30 minutes before proceeding. Preheat the oven to 110°C/225°F/Gas Mark ¼.

4 Warm the remaining olive oil in a large frying pan over a medium to high heat. Add the roulade and cook, rotating every 2 minutes, until it forms a brown crust all over, about 8 minutes total. Transfer to a chopping board and leave to rest for about 10 minutes.

5 Wrap the roulade in foil. Place, seam-side up, on a baking sheet on the centre shelf of the oven. Cook for about 2 hours, reserving any juices that accumulate. Remove from the oven and leave to rest for 15 minutes.

6 Open the foil, pour any juices into a bowl and place the meat on a chopping board. Using a serrated knife, cut into 2-cm (¾-inch) thick slices. Serve with the juices drizzled on top.

STEAK WITH FRIED EGGS

Bife à Cavalo

This simple meal is the combination of two strong proteins. It's the kind of meal that someone with a big appetite is looking for after a long day of work and exercise. Since I always have rice and beans on hand, I usually serve that as a side dish, or I serve this dish with a simple green salad and a small piece of bread, which is great for dipping in the oozing egg yolks and herbs. In Brazil, I usually make this dish using entrecôte or contrefilet (sirloin), but this recipe can be easily applied to different cuts of meat. Rib-eye steaks work well. Bringing the meat to room temperature at least 30 minutes before cooking makes it a lot easier to cook.

SERVES 4

4 x 225g (8 oz) rib-eye steaks each
sea salt and freshly ground black pepper
2 tablespoons olive oil
55g (2 oz) unsalted butter
4 eggs
1 shallot, finely chopped
2 tablespoons chopped fresh parsley
35g (1¼ oz) Parmesan shavings

1   Season the steaks with salt and pepper on both sides. Pour the oil into a large sauté pan and sauté the meat over a high heat until lightly brown and crispy on both sides, about 3 minutes per side. Remove the steaks from the pan and allow them to rest on a plate (depending on the thickness of the steak, you might need to place them in a preheated 180°C/350°F/Gas Mark 4 oven for 4–6 minutes).

2   Meanwhile, melt the butter in a medium non-stick frying pan over a medium heat. Crack each egg directly into the pan and season with salt and pepper. Cook until the egg whites are set but the yolks are still soft, about 2–3 minutes.

3   As soon as the eggs are done, place each steak on a plate and top with an egg.

4   Working fast over a medium heat, add the shallot to the leftover butter in the pan. Swirl the pan around to make sure that the shallot cooks lightly in the heat of the butter. Drizzle the shallot butter on top of each plate and garnish with the parsley and Parmesan shavings.

MEAT AND BLACK BEAN STEW
Feijoada

Feijoada is one of the most famous dishes in Brazil. Rio, my hometown, is the *feijoada* capital of Brazil, and every Saturday in Rio smells of it. This is a serious gastronomic dish, but also a simple one: a big stew of black beans with lots of different kinds of succulent meats cooked inside. It's served with white rice, *farofa* (see page 128), collard greens and orange slices. *Feijoada*, like any stew, takes a few hours to prepare, but it can handle a bit of benign neglect and still deliver an impressive result – just make sure to keep the temperature low at all times. As the beans simmer, the stew will get thicker and a glossy film should form on the top. Adjusting the consistency of the *feijoada* is easy: if it's too thick, add a little water, and if it's too thin, simmer with the pan uncovered. Feel free to season with Tabasco, Worcestershire Sauce, paprika and/or nutmeg.

1. Place the beans in a very large saucepan and cover with the cold water. Bring to the boil over a high heat. Reduce the heat to medium and cook, covered, for 1 hour, until the beans are just cooked but not too mushy. Set aside. (You can cook the beans in a pressure cooker if you want to save time, and it will only take you 15–25 minutes.)

2. Meanwhile, start preparing the meats and vegetables. Sauté the oxtail, topside and chorizo, in batches, until browned on all sides. Transfer to a large bowl and cover tightly with foil.

3. Heat the oil in a large flameproof casserole and cook the pancetta until lightly crisp. Add the onion, celery, leek, shallots, spring onions and cook, stirring occasionally, until tender, about 3–5 minutes. Add the garlic and stir to blend with the other vegetables. Add the beans and bay leaves and bring to a boil. Add the meats and any accumulated juices from the bowl. Season very lightly with salt and pepper and cover the pan. Simmer over a low heat for about 3 hours, until the meats are tender and falling off the bones. Taste and adjust the seasoning again.

4. Serve with rice, *farofa* and spring greens.

SERVES 8–10

700g (1lb 9 oz) dried black beans, picked over and rinsed

4 pieces of oxtail, about 550g (1lb 4 oz)

450g (1lb) beef topside, cut into big chunks

1 chorizo sausage, about 450g (1lb)

1 tablespoon rapeseed oil

225g (8 oz) pancetta, cut into 2.5-cm (1-inch) cubes

1 small onion, chopped

celery stick, chopped

½ leek, chopped

4 shallots, chopped

4 spring onions, chopped

2 tablespoons garlic, finely chopped

3 bay leaves

sea salt and freshly ground black pepper

CHOOSING MEAT

Pig's feet? Pig's ears? Beef cheeks? In a traditional feijoada, any piece of meat from any kind of animal (pork parts, beef parts, carne seca and linguiça are the most common) that can release a bit of flavour is thrown in the pan, even if it's just for the sake of flavour, as I do when I use pig's ears (I remove the ears just before serving). There is a world of meats beyond steaks, ribs and shoulders to explore and this is the perfect dish to venture into the land of unfamiliar cuts. Your best bet for finding these are a good butcher or ethnic shops, including Brazilian, of course. If the dish is too salty, transfer the meats from the beans. In my own interpretation of feijoada, the meats are sautéed before adding them to the beans. I think searing meats adds a great flavour.

VEAL FILET MIGNON

Filet Mignon de Vitela

In the pastry world, there are lots of caramel sauces based on caramelised sugar that is 'uncooked' with double cream, fruit juice or other liquids. In designing this unexpected recipe for catering, I thought to myself: what would happen if I caramelised sugar and uncooked it with veal stock? The sauce that resulted is the most velvety veal stock I've ever tasted. It has a light touch of sweetness, a great consistency and the most beautiful brown colour. Beef stock is an acceptable substitute, but not nearly as perfect. The filet mignon of veal is something that you don't see everywhere, and in all likelihood you'll have to special-order it from your butcher. Pork tenderloin is a good substitute. Although endives are often found in salad mixes or raw hors d'oeuvres, they take a completely different turn when cooked. The texture changes from crisp to creamy, and the bitterness changes to mild and sweet. Fennel is a more solid alternative.

SERVES 4

475ml (17fl oz) veal stock (see page 113)
200g (7 oz) plus 1 tablespoon sugar
2 tablespoons water
60ml (2fl oz) double cream
sea salt and freshly ground black pepper
⅛ teaspoon freshly squeezed lemon juice

4 endives, about 450g (1lb) in total
15g (½ oz) unsalted butter
1 tablespoon sugar

2 veal or pork tenderloin steaks, 675g (1½lb) in total
2 tablespoons rapeseed oil

---

1 For the sauce, bring the veal stock to a simmer in a medium saucepan.

2 Place the sugar and water in another large saucepan and cook over a high heat until the sugar turns a dark amber caramel colour, about 2–3 minutes. Add the stock all at once. Reduce the heat to low and simmer until it reduces by half and thickens, about 15 minutes.

3 Add the double cream, whisk lightly and cook the sauce until the cream is well blended, about 2 minutes. Season with salt, pepper and the lemon juice. This can be prepared up to 3 days ahead of time and kept in the refrigerator in an airtight plastic container.

4 Prepare the endives by removing any limp outer leaves, then slice the endives in half lengthways. Place in a large frying pan with the butter. Add 175ml (6fl oz) water and

season with salt and pepper. Cook, partly covered, over a low heat until tender, about 5 minutes. Uncover the pan to allow any remaining water to evaporate (but make sure the endives don't dry out), about 3 minutes.

5 Using a pair of tongs, carefully lift the endives so that you can add the sugar to the bottom of the pan. Cook until the sugar starts to caramelise. Add another 60ml (2fl oz) water and turn the heat to high, swirling the pan around and making sure that the endives are lightly coated. Cook until the liquid evaporates. Season with salt and pepper and keep warm.

6 Preheat the oven to 190°C/375°F/Gas Mark 5. Trim any silver skin from the meat and season.

7 Heat the oil in an ovenproof frying pan over a medium heat and swirl to coat the base. Add the meat and cook until golden brown, about 6 minutes. Place the pan in the oven to finish cooking the meat until it's medium done, about 5–6 minutes. Remove from the oven and leave to rest for 5 minutes before slicing.

8 Cut the meat on the diagonal across the grain into 1-cm (½-inch) thick slices. Place an endive and a few slices of tenderloin on a warm plate, and top everything with the caramel sauce.

GRILLED CACHAÇA MARINATED FLANK STEAK

Fraldinha Marinada na Cachaça e Grelhada

This is a great recipe for grilling. The marinade has a real wow factor, as the cachaça adds a unique spicy flavour to the steak. If you cannot find cachaça, vodka also works. Marinades are one of my favourite ways to tenderise meats and they add tons of flavour. Keep in mind that with all marinades time is your best ally. If you can marinate the meat for 2–3 days, then do so – it will only make the taste even better. I have also prepared lamb using this marinade and it turned out wonderfully.

SERVES 2–4

1 medium onion, thinly sliced

3 garlic cloves, roughly chopped

1 teaspoon tomato ketchup

1 teaspoon coriander seeds

1 tablespoon honey

1 teaspoon soy sauce

60ml (2fl oz) cachaça

125ml (4fl oz) rapeseed or olive oil

1 flank steak, about 450g (1lb)

sea salt and freshly ground black pepper

1 In a large bowl, whisk together the first 8 ingredients. Place the meat in a large zip-lock plastic bag and pour the marinade into the bag. Rub the marinade around the meat until it is well distributed. Remove all the air from the plastic bag and seal it well. Place the meat in the refrigerator in such a position so that it is covered by the marinade and leave for at least 12 hours, preferably 2–3 days.

2 Preheat a gas barbecue on high heat for at least 10 minutes before cooking. Remove the meat from the marinade and wipe off the remaining specks of onion, garlic and coriander.

3 Season the meat with salt and pepper on both sides and place it on the hot grill. If you want to create attractive crosshatch grill marks, cook for 2 minutes and rotate the meat 45 degrees from its original position, then cook for another 2 minutes; do this on each side. Depending on the thickness of the meat, leave it cooking on the barbecue for 4–5 minutes on each side, turning sides once. If you like your meat rare or well done, adjust the cooking time according to your taste (see below). A meat thermometer is always a good tool when seeking precisely the right degree of doneness.

FLANK STEAK TEMPERATURE GUIDELINES

Blue – 49°C/120°F

Rare – 52°C/125°F

Medium rare – 57°C/135°F

Medium – 63°C/145°F

Medium Well – 68°C/155°F

Well done – 77°C/170°F

BRAZILIAN BEEF RAGU

Picadinho

2 tablespoons vegetable or rapeseed oil
900g (2lb) beef shoulder, cut into 5-mm (¼-inch) pieces
sea salt and freshly ground black pepper
2 tablespoons olive oil
40g (1½ oz) pancetta, cut into 5-mm (¼-inch) pieces
1 small onion, finely chopped
3 spring onions (white and green parts), finely chopped
about ⅔ cup red pepper, finely chopped
about ⅔ cup yellow pepper, finely chopped
about ⅔ cup green pepper, finely chopped
5 cloves garlic, finely minced
175ml (6fl oz) red wine, such as Cabernet Sauvignon or Zinfandel
2 tablespoons tomato purée
475ml (17fl oz) veal stock (see page 113)
2 teaspoons Worcestershire sauce
pinch of ground nutmeg
pinch of cayenne pepper
2 plum tomatoes, peeled, deseeded and diced
3 tablespoons chopped fresh parsley

Picadinho is a staple of Brazilian cooking much like Bolognese is in Italian cuisine. Cut the peppers very small, as you want them to almost disappear while cooking, but their sweetness will be impossible to ignore. Feel free to use different kinds of meat like lamb and veal. In Brazil, they don't use bacon or pancetta to make *picadinho*, but I think it adds immense flavour to the dish. You can serve *picadinho* with pasta, or with rice or mashed potatoes. If you want to really hold to Brazilian tradition, you can serve it with *farofa* (see page 128).

1   Heat the oil in a large heavy-based saucepan over a high heat. Season the beef with salt and pepper and add to the pan, in batches if necessary to avoid overcrowding and cook until cooked through, about 3–5 minutes. Transfer to a bowl and cover with foil so that no steam escapes.

2   Place the olive oil and pancetta in the same pan. Cook over a medium heat, stirring, until lightly crispy, about 2–3 minutes.

3   Reduce the heat to low and add the onion, spring onions, and peppers. Cook, stirring frequently, until the vegetables become soft and tender, about 3 minutes. Add the garlic and cook, stirring, for another minute.

4   Transfer the beef and all accumulated juices to the pan and stir. Pour in the wine and simmer until it has reduced by a little more than half, about 5 minutes. Add the tomato purée, veal stock and Worcestershire sauce. Season lightly with salt, pepper and the nutmeg and cayenne. Cover and simmer over very low heat for about 1–1½ hours.

5   Adjust the seasoning, add the tomatoes and simmer for 3 minutes. Spoon the *picadinho* over your starch of choice and garnish with the parsley.

BEEF MINCE AND CREAMY SWEETCORN PIE

Torta de Carne e Pamonha

Strongly rooted in indigenous cooking and similar to tomales in Mexico, *pamonha* is a paste made from puréed sweetcorn and milk, which is wrapped and steamed inside corn husks. In Brazil, this street food is prepared either sweet with sugar and cinnamon or savoury with cheese. I was inspired to create a Brazilian version of shepherd's pie when I recently ate a savoury *pamonha* in Brazil and realised that a creamy and cheesy sweetcorn crust would be the perfect topping for a layer of beef mince. I first developed this recipe in Brazil, using fresh corn, dry polenta, milk and Parmesan for the topping. I was later inspired by the Mexican combination of Cheddar over minced meats and chillies and the pie tastes even better this way. This can be prepared well ahead of serving.

2 tablespoons olive oil

115g (4 oz) pancetta, finely diced

1 small onion, chopped

4 spring onions, chopped

1 carrot, chopped

1 celery stick, chopped

2 garlic cloves, chopped

550g (1lb 4 oz) beef mince

80ml (2⅔fl oz) white wine

125ml (4fl oz) tomato purée

225ml (8fl oz) full-fat milk

225ml (8fl oz) water

sea salt and freshly ground black pepper

2 tablespoons chopped fresh parsley

115g (4 oz) sweetcorn kernels

25g (1 oz) unsalted butter

1 tablespoon baking powder

140g (5 oz) polenta

225ml (8fl oz) soured cream

175g (6 oz) grated Cheddar, divided

18 x 28-cm (7 x 11-inch) baking dish

1   Heat the olive oil in a large, heavy-based saucepan over a medium to high heat and add the pancetta. Cook, stirring, until lightly crisp, about 3 minutes. Add the onion, spring onions, carrots and celery and cook, stirring frequently, until soft and tender, about 3 minutes. Add the garlic and cook for another minute. Add the beef mince to the pan and break the meat into tiny bits until completely cooked through, about 6–8 minutes.

2   Add the wine and reduce by half, about 3 minutes. Add the tomato purée, milk and water. Stir gently and cook, partly covered, for 1 hour over a low heat.

3   Season with salt and pepper and sprinkle with the parsley. Transfer to the baking dish, spread with a spatula and leave to cool at room temperature.

4   Meanwhile, place the sweetcorn in the bowl of a food processor and purée into a smooth paste.

5   Melt the butter in a medium saucepan over a low heat. Add the polenta and mix until the polenta becomes slightly wet. Add the puréed sweetcorn and stir over a low heat until it looks like a coarse meal, about 1 minute. Immediately transfer to a large bowl.

6   Add the baking powder and mix well. Add the soured cream and 115g (4 oz) of the cheese, and mash everything together until it forms a dough. Season with salt and pepper.

7   Preheat the oven to 190°C/375°F/Gas Mark 5. Spread the dough on top of the meat layer with a spatula, making sure that the meat layer is all covered.

8   Sprinkle the remaining Cheddar cheese on top. Bake the pie in the oven until the cheese is bubbling and the top is golden brown, about 20–25 minutes.

9   Remove from the oven and leave to rest at room temperature for 10 minutes before serving.

LAMB STEW WITH YUCCA AND TURMERIC

Cozido de Carneiro, Aipim e Açafrão-da-Terra

Although Brazil is generally hot, when it comes to comfort foods, we inherited a taste for stews. This recipe is inspired by the flavours of Goiás, located in the centre of Brazil, where they use lots of lamb, yucca and turmeric. The yucca infuses the stock with a uniquely earthy element. I recommend using veal stock, but if you have access to homemade or fresh-from-the-butcher lamb stock, go for that. Lamb shoulder is my favourite cut of meat because it is tender and full of flavour, but a leg of lamb is fine, too.

SERVES 6–8

1.3kg (3lb) lamb shoulder, fat trimmed, cut into 4–5-cm (1½–2-inch) pieces
sea salt and freshly ground black pepper
2 yuccas (about 225g (8 oz) each)
4 tablespoons olive oil
125ml (4fl oz) white wine
2 medium onions, finely chopped
3 small carrots, peeled and cut into large chunks
2 celery sticks, cut into large chunks
10 garlic cloves, finely chopped
2 teaspoons turmeric
1 litre (1¾ pints) veal stock (see page 113)
¼ cup chopped fresh coriander

1 Place the meat on a tray and season with salt and pepper. Cover loosely with clingfilm and let come to room temperature.

2 Prepare the yucca as on page 32 up until step 2 and drain.

3 Pour 2 tablespoons of the olive oil into a large, heavy-based saucepan and swirl to coat the entire base. Add the lamb and cook, in batches, over a medium heat, until browned, about 3–5 minutes. Transfer to a bowl and cover with foil.

4 Add the wine to the pan and bring to a full boil, then pour it over the meat and cover the bowl again.

5 Wipe the pan and add the remaining 2 tablespoons olive oil. Stir in the chopped onions, carrots and celery. Cook until soft, about 3 minutes. Stir in the garlic and cook for another minute. Stir in the tumeric. Add the lamb with all juices that have accumulated in the bowl. Add the veal stock, enough to cover the pieces of meat and vegetables, and bring to the boil, then reduce the heat to low.

6 Add the yucca pieces to the pan. Simmer gently, either on the hob or in a 150°C/300°F/Gas Mark 2 oven until the meat is very tender and the yucca is cooked but not mushy, about 2½–3 hours. Turn off the heat and let the stew settle for a few minutes.

7 Discard the chunks of carrot and celery. Season with salt and pepper and garnish with the fresh coriander.

DUCK RICE

Arroz de Pato

I eat duck rice quite often in Brazil. It's a classic Portuguese dish sometimes prepared in the style of fried rice, other times prepared in the style of risotto. I could never really pick which was my favourite way – until I dined at Aldea, Portuguese Chef Georges Mendez's new restaurant. When the duck rice arrived, I felt like culture was singing to me. In his version, Chef Mendez prepares the dish using a paella technique. Mixed in with the rice are shredded meat from a duck confit, thinly sliced chorizo and black olives. This version is inspired by Chef Mendez's, but I took a real short cut here by using shop-bought duck confit. It's a step that takes you there just a little faster than if you were making your own.

SERVES 4

2 confit of duck legs

3 tablespoons extra virgin olive oil

1 small and thin chorizo sausage, about 115g (4 oz), cut on the diagonal into thin slices

700ml (1 ¼ pints) chicken stock

½ medium onion, finely chopped

3 garlic cloves, finely chopped

pinch of saffron threads

½ teaspoon paprika

1 plum tomato, peeled, deseeded and diced

200g (7 oz) paella rice

sea salt and freshly ground black pepper

25g (1 oz) Kalamata olives, stoned and sliced

1. Preheat the oven to 190°C/375°F/Gas Mark 5.

2. Warm the duck legs and fat gently in a frying pan over a low heat. Separate the legs from the fat and leave to cool to room temperature. Use your fingers to shred the meat and save the fat for other uses. Set aside.

3. Heat 1 tablespoon of the olive oil in a small sauté pan, add the chorizo and cook until lightly browned, about 2 minutes. Transfer to a plate, cover with foil and set aside.

4. Bring the stock to a simmer in a saucepan.

5. Heat the remaining olive oil in a large frying pan over a medium heat. Add the onion and garlic and cook until slightly golden. Add the saffron and paprika and cook for another minute. Stir in the diced tomato and cook until soft, about 2 minutes. Add the rice and stir well to coat in the oil, making sure that it's spread evenly around the pan. Add the stock and bring to the boil. Season lightly with salt and pepper.

6. Add the duck meat and chorizo and stir just once (if you stir later in the process, the rice becomes sticky). Place the frying pan in the oven and cook until the rice is cooked but not mushy, about 8–10 minutes.

7. Remove the frying pan from the oven. Taste and adjust the seasoning, mix in the olives and serve hot.

CHICKEN STOCK Caldo de Galinha

450–900g (1–2lb) chicken bones (from any part of the chicken)
1 onion, peeled and quartered
1 carrot, peeled and cut into chunks
1 celery stick, cut into chunks
2 garlic cloves, peeled
1 teaspoon back peppercorns, cracked
a few thyme sprigs
a few parsley sprigs
2–3 bay leaves

1 Remove the excess fat from the bones (especially if you are starting with raw bones). Place them in a large saucepan and cover with cold water above the bones. Don't try to add too much water or the stock will be too watery and lack flavour. Bring to the boil over a high heat. At this point change the water if it's bloody, or continue by reducing the heat to low and simmer over a very gentle heat for about 30 minutes, skimming the foam occasionally.

2 Add the vegetables and herbs and simmer for another 15 minutes, skimming occasionally.

3 Taste the stock. When it has a rich chicken flavour, remove the bones and vegetables with a slotted spoon and strain the stock, first through a medium sieve, then through a fine-mesh sieve.

4 Place the stock over an ice bath, then chill in the refrigerator for 12–24 hours – chilled is the best way to judge the quality of the stock. The more gelatinous, the better. Carefully remove any fat that has accumulated on the top and discard it. Divide the stock into several small plastic containers, label them and store in the refrigerator for up to 4 days or in the freezer for up to 4 months.

SHRIMP STOCK Caldo de Camarão

2 tablespoons olive oil
shells from 900g (2lb) prawns
1 large onion, peeled and quartered
1 celery stick, cut into chunks
1 small carrot, peeled and cut into chunks
3 garlic cloves, peeled
2 bay leaves
a few thyme sprigs
a few parsley sprigs

1 Heat the oil in a large, heavy-based saucepan over a medium heat. Add the shells and cook until they turn bright pink, about 3–5 minutes. Add the vegetables and cook until they start to soften, another 2–3 minutes.

2 Pour water until just slightly above the shells, then reduce the heat to low. Add the herbs and simmer over a very low heat for about 30 minutes, skimming the foam occasionally.

3 Remove the shells and vegetables with a slotted spoon and strain through a fine-mesh sieve. Place the stock over an ice bath, then chill in the refrigerator. Divide the stock into several small plastic containers, label them and store in the refrigerator for up to 2 days or in the freezer for up to 3 months.

VEAL STOCK Caldo de Vitela

2.7kg (6lb) veal bones
3 carrots, peeled and cut into chunks
2 onions, peeled and quartered
5 garlic cloves, peeled
60ml (2fl oz) tomato purée
1 tablespoon black peppercorns, cracked
a few thyme sprigs
a few parsley sprigs
3–4 bay leaves

1   Preheat the oven to 230°C/450°F/Gas Mark 8. Place the veal bones in a large roasting tin, but do not overcrowd them. Roast until medium brown on one side, about 30 minutes, then turn them upside down (remove any accumulated fat at this point) and continue to roast for another 30 minutes.

2   Transfer the bones to a large saucepan and cover them with cold water to just 2.5-cm (1–2 inches) above the bones. Cover and cook over a high heat just to bring to the boil, about 15 minutes. Uncover, reduce the heat to low and cook at a very gentle simmer, skimming the foam occasionally. Do not try to rush the process by raising the heat and boiling. You want very small bubbles at the most.

3   When the bones have cooked for about 4 hours, add the vegetables, tomato purée, peppercorns and herbs. Continue to simmer or another 2 hours, skimming occasionally.

4   Remove the big bones from the pan with a slotted spoon and strain the stock, first through a medium sieve, then through a fine-mesh sieve. Place the stock over an ice bath, then chill in the refrigerator for 12–24 hours. Carefully discard any fat that has accumulated on the top. Divide the stock into several small plastic containers, label them and store in the refrigerator for up to 4 days or in the freezer for up to 6 months.

Side Dishes
Acompanhamentos

RICE AND BEANS

Arroz e Feijão

Brazil is a rice and bean nation. This duo is the backbone of every household in the country. When it comes to the basics, Brazilians count on ordinary white rice. I like basmati and jasmine, and you can use either one for this recipe. Brazilians like their rice quite loose, never sticky, and that's why we wash it beforehand. We also never stir during the cooking process. As for the beans, black beans rule in Brazil, but feel free to use other types of beans such as red kidney or pinto. When looking for a meaty or smoky flavour in your beans, you can add bacon or sausage. The flavour of cooked beans does improve after a day or two in the refrigerator. The beans cook in two easy steps. First, in the pressure cooker. Second, in a regular saucepan with onions, garlic and seasonings. One pot of cooked beans can last for 3–4 days and it's definitely something you can make ahead of time. They tend to get creamier when resting in the refrigerator, so by all means adjust the consistency by adding a little water or stock.

SERVES 6–8

400g (14 oz) white long-grain rice, such as basmati
2 teaspoons sea salt
4 tablespoons extra virgin olive oil
2 garlic cloves, chopped, plus 1 tablespoon, finely chopped
450g (1 lb) dried black beans, picked over and rinsed (but not soaked)
1 medium onion, finely chopped
sea salt and freshly ground black pepper
3 fresh bay leaves
1–2 teaspoons Worcestershire sauce

1 Rinse the rice in cold water to wash away the excess starch.

2 Bring 750ml (25½fl oz) of water, the rice, salt, 2 tablespoons of the olive oil and the 2 chopped garlic cloves to boil in a heavy-based saucepan, tightly covered. Reduce the heat to a gentle simmer and cook, covered, until the rice is tender and the water is absorbed, about 15–20 minutes.

3 Remove from the heat and leave to stand, uncovered, for 5 minutes. Fluff up with a fork.

4 Place the black beans in a pressure cooker and cover with cold water by 5cm (2 inches). Lock the lid and bring to the boil. When you hear the sound of the pressure cooker in full gear, reduce the heat to medium-low. (It is very important to maintain a constant gentle pressure because the pressure keeps increasing as the boiling point of the water

increases.) Check the beans after 25–30 minute – they should be tender but not mushy. The water will be dark but still clear. Remove from the heat and set aside.

5 Pour the remaining 2 tablespoons olive oil into a saucepan and cook the onion over a medium heat until soft, about 3 minutes. Add the tablespoon finely chopped garlic and cook until golden brown, about 2 minutes. Immediately pour the beans and liquid into the pan, then add salt, pepper and the bay leaves. Simmer the beans over a gentle heat until the liquid becomes thicker and glossy, about 15–20 minutes. Check the seasoning and add the Worcestershire sauce to taste. Serve over the rice.

PRESSURE COOKERS

Pressure cookers have a relevant cultural value in Brazil; as they symbolise the importance of beans. They are used every day and make life a lot easier, reducing cooking time from 2 hours in a regular pan to just 30–40 minutes. The idea behind a pressure cooker is that no air or liquid can escape, creating pressure and making cooking a lot faster. Never open a pressure cooker without releasing the pressure first. To do this, lift up the centre handle until all the steam – or pressure – is released. You can also place the pan under running water. Read the instructions for your appliance before using, as each brand may differ slightly.

THREE BEAN RISOTTO

Risotto de Três Feijões

This intriguing risotto is a creative way to serve one of the most internationally loved comfort foods with Brazilian flair. You want the proper risotto texture: creamy rice that is wet, loose and runny, not thick and pasty. Then add the flavours of Brazil with *carne seca* and beans. Although I am using three different kinds of beans, feel free to use more or fewer varieties, and I use canned to save you time. If you are left with extra beans, use them in soups, salads, casseroles or stews. As for the dried beef, you can use bacon or pancetta as substitutes. Note that the dried beef is not being desalted, so it will infuse the risotto with plenty of saltiness. Try to use a low-sodium chicken stock and taste the risotto before adding any additional seasoning. This flexible dish can be served as an appetiser, main course or a side dish.

SERVES 4

850ml (1½ pints) chicken stock (see page 112)
1 tablespoon extra virgin olive oil, plus
   extra to garnish
55g (2 oz) *carne seca* (dried beef), finely diced
½ medium onion, finely diced
200g (7 oz) Arborio rice
2 tablespoons dry white wine
2 tablespoons tinned black beans, rinsed
2 tablespoons tinned red kidney beans, rinsed
2 tablespoons tinned borlotti beans, rinsed
25g (1 oz) unsalted butter
sea salt and freshly ground black pepper
2 tablespoons chopped fresh tarragon

1   In a medium saucepan, bring the chicken stock to a simmer.

2   Heat the olive oil in a large, heavy-based saucepan over a medium heat and add the dried beef. Cook, stirring occasionally, until the meat browns and turns lightly crisp, about 3 minutes. Add the onion and cook, stirring frequently, until soft and translucent, about 2 minutes. Add the rice and stir frequently until the grains are warm and coated with the onion and meat mixture, about 3 minutes. Add the wine and simmer, stirring constantly, until the liquid is absorbed, about 1 minute.

3   Slowly add one ladle of simmering stock and allow the rice to cook, stirring often, until the liquid is absorbed. Adjust the heat to maintain a gentle simmer. Add another ladle and repeat the process. Continue adding ladles of stock only when the previous addition has been completely absorbed. Cook until the rice is tender but still firm to the bite, about 18–20 minutes. Season lightly with salt if necessary.

4   Add the beans and butter and fold into the rice. Don't let the risotto get too thick; if the rice seems to have absorbed all of the liquid, add another tablespoon of chicken stock to achieve the right creamy consistency. Taste the dish, checking flavour and doneness.

5   Sprinkle the tarragon over the risotto and spoon it onto warm plates. Serve immediately while the risotto is still hot.

EGG STUFFED BAKED POTATO

Batatas Recheadas com Ovo

The potatoes in this recipe are served whole: stuffed with mashed potatoes, topped with an egg, drenched in double cream, and dusted with Parmesan cheese. So many textures and tastes – crunchy, smooth, rich, buttery, salty, custardy, cheesy – all in one dish. Not to mention that you get those extra vitamins from the skin. I like to serve these potatoes with the yolks very runny, but feel free to cook for a few more minutes for a firmer yolk. This is the perfect side dish for a chicken or beef dish; or it can serve as the main course with a green salad. Make sure you buy potatoes of the same size and with a nice oval shape.

MAKES 4 SERVINGS

4 medium floury potatoes, such as Desiree
70g (2½ oz) unsalted butter at room temperature
75ml (2½fl oz) full-fat milk, hot
4 large eggs
4 teaspoons double cream
4 tablespoons freshly grated Parmesan
sea salt and freshly ground black pepper
pinch of freshly grated nutmeg

---

1 Preheat the oven to 180°C/350°F/Gas Mark 4.

2 Wash the potatoes in cold water and rub the skin to remove any dirt. Dry each potato with kitchen paper. Place them in the oven and bake the potatoes until tender and a knife inserted into the centre goes in easily, about 30–40 minutes.

3 Remove from the oven and, while they are still hot, cut off the top horizontally, following the oval shape of the potato. Using a tea towel to hold the hot potato, scoop out most of the potato flesh with a spoon, leaving the sides and the bottom with a thin layer of potato to hold its shape. Place the scooped potato through a ricer or food mill.

4 Add the butter and mix well. Add the hot milk, a little at a time, and mix until well blended. Season with salt, pepper and the nutmeg.

5 Transfer the mashed potatoes to a piping bag or zip-lock plastic bag and cut off the tip. Fill the baked potatoes halfway with the mashed potato mixture, leaving space for the egg. You may have some extra mashed potatoes left in the piping bag.

6 One at a time, break the 4 eggs and carefully remove about a tablespoon of the egg whites with a spoon and discard. Pour each remaining egg intact inside each potato. Season with salt and pepper.

7 Add 1 teaspoon of double cream to each potato and sprinkle 1 tablespoon Parmesan on top. Bake the potatoes until the egg whites are just set but the yolks are still runny, about 6–8 minutes.

ROASTED POTATOES WITH BAY LEAVES

Batatinhas Assadas com Louro

While the French use a lot of duck fat to make confits, Brazilians make good use of chicken fat. Fast and easy to prepare, it pairs perfectly with young potatoes. I never pass up the opportunity to make rendered fat from chicken skin (see below). I end up with a batch of crackling that is irresistible to snack on. If you don't want to make chicken fat, feel free to use duck fat, which is a lot easier to find. The combination of potatoes and bay leaves is classic in Brazil and Portugal, but you could also use rosemary or thyme. I love to serve it with grilled meat (such as the Marinated Flank Steak/Cachaça on page 106).

SERVES 4

675g (1lb 8 oz) small, yellow-fleshed potatoes
55g (2 oz) chicken fat, melted and cooled
6 large garlic cloves, peeled and left whole
10 bay leaves (preferably fresh)
sea salt and freshly ground black pepper

MAKING CHICKEN (OR DUCK) FAT

Trim off the skin and fat from 1 whole chicken (or duck). Cut into medium pieces and put into a heavy-based saucepan. Cook, uncovered, over a low heat. As the fat begins to melt, strain it through a colander into a bowl and return the skin pieces to continue cooking over a low heat until they are crisp and have released all of their fat. Strain the clear liquid through a sieve and leave to cool. You will have 125–175ml (4–6fl oz) from a chicken; 225–300ml (8–10fl oz) from a duck. Store in an airtight plastic container for up to 6 weeks in the refrigerator or 3 months in the freezer.

1 Preheat the oven to 190°C/375°F/Gas Mark 5.

2 Wash the potatoes in cold water and scrub the skin to remove any dirt. Dry with kitchen paper and cut the potatoes into large chunks.

3 Place the potatoes in a large bowl and pour the chicken fat over. Stir carefully with a rubber spatula, making sure that each potato chunk is well coated with fat.

4 Add the garlic cloves and bay leaves. Season with salt and pepper and stir again.

5 Place the potatoes in a large roasting tin in the oven. Bake until they are tender and golden brown, about 30–35 minutes, stirring the potatoes every 10 minutes.

SPRING GREENS

Couve Mineira Refogada

Collard greens may be Brazil's most popular green vegetable, and an obligatory side dish served with *feijoada*. Vegetables in Brazil are seldom just steamed and collard greens are no exception. Onions and garlic are always present as the basic accompaniments, but collards work well with a range of seasonings and make an excellent addition to pasta sauces, soups, and egg dishes. In place of collard greens, use spring greens, choosing dark green ones with firm stems and no discolourations. Unlike other vegetables that turn into mush when overcooked, greens are very forgiving – it's quite hard to overcook them. If you like them crispy, just toss the leaves in some oil with onion. When you add liquid, you lose brightness but gain tenderness. In this recipe, I suggest braising with a small quantity of water, but feel free to add any kind of stock instead, and even a piece of smoked meat to oomph the flavour.

SERVES 4

1 bunch of spring greens, about 675–900g
2 tablespoons extra virgin olive oil
½ onion, finely chopped
sea salt and freshly ground black pepper

1   Trim the stems and the thick centre ribs from the spring green leaves. Choose some of the thickest stems; peel them to remove the thick fibre and chop them roughly. Set aside.

2   Stack a few leaves and roll them tightly into a cigar shape. Cut them into very thin strips crossways and place in a bowl. Repeat with the remaining leaves.

3   Pour the olive oil into a large saucepan. Add the onion and cook over a medium heat, stirring occasionally, until soft and translucent, about 2 minutes. Add the greens and toss them, making sure that all the leaves are well coated with the oil and onion mixture. Season with salt and pepper. Add 225ml (8fl oz) of water, cover the pan and reduce the heat to low. Simmer gently until the leaves are soft, about 10 minutes. Drain any excess liquid before serving.

CARROTS WITH PINEAPPLE SAUCE AND SULTANAS

Cenoura com Molho de Abacaxi e Passas

This recipe is inspired by the wonderful salads I used to eat at Celeiro, a restaurant famous in Rio for just that. When marinated in a pineapple and raisin sauce, shredded carrots become crunchy and tender, receiving both sweet and sour notes. The three ingredients harmonise nicely and the result is very refreshing and healthy. Try to use a fresh and fragrant pineapple and organic and crispy carrots for this recipe. Feel free to use raisins instead of sultanas if that's what you prefer. Bring this to a barbecue instead of potato salad or coleslaw, and be prepared for compliments!

SERVES 4

350g (12 oz) finely diced fresh pineapple
75ml (2½fl oz) water
55g (2 oz) sultanas
2 teaspoons Dijon mustard
1 teaspoon white wine vinegar
sea salt and freshly ground black pepper
pinch of turmeric
pinch of ground cinnamon
350g (12 oz) carrots (about 4–5), peeled and trimmed
2 tablespoons mayonnaise
3 tablespoons chopped fresh chives

1 Place half the pineapple with the water in a blender and blend until the fruit is completely liquefied, about 2 minutes. Strain the juice through a fine sieve into a measuring jug and keep 225ml (8fl oz). If need be, press the pulp to extract more juice, then discard the pulp.

2 Bring the pineapple juice to a simmer in a medium saucepan over a low heat Add the remaining diced pineapple, sultanas, mustard and vinegar. Cook over a very low heat, stirring occasionally, until the sultanas soften and the mustard dissolves in the juice, about 3–5 minutes. Season with salt and pepper and the turmeric and cinnamon. Transfer to a bowl and leave to cool.

3 Meanwhile, grate the carrots using the largest holes in your grater. Place the grated carrots in a bowl.

4 When the pineapple sauce is cooled, fold in the mayonnaise with a rubber spatula. Pour the pineapple sauce over the carrots and fold everything together.

5 Chill the salad in the refrigerator for at least 1 hour. Remove it from the refrigerator at least 20 minutes before serving. Garnish with the chopped fresh chives.

ASPARAGUS WITH SHALLOT AND PARSLEY SAUCE

Asparagus com Molho de Echalote e Salsinha

This dish is a light and elegant side dish for meat or fish. In Brazil, fresh asparagus is considered a fancy vegetable and the herb-shallot sauce only elevates its bright, fresh flavour. When I can, I like to mix white and green asparagus, but when I don't have the white on hand, I use fresh hearts of palm. Both taste wonderful with this sauce.

SERVES 4

450g (1lb) fresh asparagus spears
3 tablespoons salt
¼ teaspoon bicarbonate of soda
1 tablespoon olive oil
1 rasher of bacon, finely chopped
2 small shallots, finely chopped
225ml (8fl oz) chicken stock
25g (1 oz) unsalted butter, chilled, cut into pieces
sea salt and freshly ground black pepper
2 tablespoons chopped fresh parsley
25g (1 oz) freshly grated Parmesan

1   Cut the woody ends off the asparagus and peel, leaving the tips intact.

2   Bring a large saucepan of water to the boil. Add the salt and bicarbonate of soda. Submerge the asparagus in the water and cook until they just become soft. Immediately transfer them to an ice bath and then let them cool completely. Remove from the ice bath and let them dry on kitchen paper.

3   In a medium sauté pan, add the olive oil and bacon and cook over a medium heat until lightly crisp, about 2 minutes. Reduce the heat and add the shallots, stirring occasionally, being careful not to brown them, about 2 minutes. Add the chicken stock and reduce by half, about 5 minutes.

4   Lift the saucepan a little way above the heat and add the cold pieces of butter. Shake the pan back and forth until the butter is melted and incorporated into the sauce. Season with salt and pepper. Add the asparagus to the pan and reheat over a very low heat, being careful not to boil the sauce. Add the parsley.

5   Transfer the asparagus and sauce to a plate and serve with the Parmesan sprinkled on top.

BROCCOLI AND MINAS CHEESE SOUFFLÉ

Suflê de Brócolis e Queijo Minas

This is a different kind of soufflé, one that can withstand a 24-hour resting period easily because the egg whites are not whipped. Whole eggs are added to a healthy and refreshing broccoli and Minas base. You can also substitute brocollini or broccoli rabe. They all come from the same family but have different degrees of bitterness, from the mildest broccoli to the most bitter broccoli rabe (which is great to pair with sausages). In Brazil we often serve soufflés as a side dish for protein, but feel free to serve it as a lunch or a light dinner with a green salad. I like to bake these in individual ramekins, 120ml (4fl oz) in size.

SERVES 6–8

500ml (17fl oz) whole milk

85g (3 oz) butter, plus extra, melted, for greasing

6 tablespoons plain flour

sea salt and freshly ground pepper

pinch of ground nutmeg

pinch of cayenne pepper

5 whole eggs

225g (8 oz) grated Minas cheese

200g (7 oz) chopped cooked broccoli

25g (1 oz) grated Parmesan

---

1 Preheat the oven to 190°C/375°F/Gas Mark 5. Lightly coat the insides of the ramekins with melted butter.

2 Bring the milk to a light simmer in a small saucepan.

3 Melt the butter in a medium saucepan over a low heat. Add the flour, whisk well and cook until it's blended, about 1 minute. Add the warm milk all at once and whisk well until it's a smooth béchamel sauce. Season with salt and pepper and the nutmeg and cayenne. Transfer to a bowl and leave to cool at room temperature for 10–15 minutes.

4 Break all the eggs into a small bowl, season with a small pinch of salt and pepper and lightly whisk them together.

5 Add the eggs to the béchamel sauce and whisk well until completely smooth. Add the Minas cheese and broccoli and fold everything together with a rubber spatula.

6 Pour the batter inside the prepared ramekins, about three-quarters full. Sprinkle the Parmesan on top of each. Place the ramekins on a baking sheet and bake until they are puffed and lightly golden brown, about 15–20 minutes.

7 Remove the ramekins from the oven and serve immediately.

TOASTED MANIOC FLOUR WITH EGGS AND SPRING ONIONS

Farofa de Ovo e Cebolinha

Farofa is the term for a side dish using toasted *farinha de mandioca* – in English, manioc flour, which is a dried flour similar in looks and texture to breadcrumbs, made from yucca (see the Glossary on page 170). The making of *farofa* as a dish couldn't be easier. It is plain manioc flour toasted in butter. A few of the classic *farofa* dishes include eggs and spring onions, eggs and bacon, banana, peppers and dendê oil, green beans and carrots, peas and sweetcorn, and so on and so forth. *Farofa* can be extremely dry, since the manioc flour immediately sucks up all the juices from anything it encounters, especially when it's served plain. The trick to making a moist *farofa* is to use a small amount of manioc flour in proportion to the other components, turning a side dish into a savoury accompaniment so tempting, you may even forget there is a main course.

SERVES 4

25g (1 oz) unsalted butter
275g (9½ oz) manioc flour
2 tablespoons extra virgin olive oil
4 spring onions (white and green parts), thinly sliced on the diagonal
5 large eggs
sea salt and freshly ground black pepper

1 Melt the butter in a medium saucepan over a low heat. Add the manioc flour and toast it to a light golden colour, stirring often, about 8–10 minutes. Make sure you stir constantly, otherwise the flour will burn. Set aside.

2 Reserve a few slices of spring onion for garnish. In a non-stick frying pan, warm the olive oil over a medium heat and cook the spring onions until they just start to soften.

3 Whisk the eggs in a small bowl and season with salt and pepper. Pour the eggs into the spring onions and scramble them lightly, being careful not to overcook them. Add the toasted manioc flour and stir everything together. Season with salt and pepper.

4 Pour into a serving dish and garnish with the reserved spring onions.

Desserts
Sobremesas

CHOCOLATE BRIGADERIOS

Brigadeiro de Chocolate

Chewy, fudgy, addictive. These little chocolate fudge balls are as common and as loved in Brazil as cookies and brownies are in the United States. Traditionally, *brigadeiros* are a simple mixture of condensed milk, sweetened cocoa powder and butter, cooked to a fudge state, then formed into little balls and rolled in chocolate sprinkles. I find this to be much too sweet, so I have made a few changes to the original recipe, adding real chocolate, real cocoa, double cream and corn syrup. Chocolate sprinkles are usually made with vegetable fat, so unless I know the sprinkle is made with real chocolate like the ones from Guittard or Cacao Barry, I prefer to use cocoa powder, or grated chocolate, for rolling and the result is amazing. This is a perfect dessert to give as a gift for any occasion. Children will love it and so will adults.

MAKES ABOUT 45 BRIGADERIOS

2 x 397g (14 oz) tins sweetened condensed milk
55g (2 oz) unsalted butter
2 tablespoons double cream
2 teaspoons light corn syrup
90g (3¼ oz) dark chocolate, chopped
2 teaspoons unsweetened cocoa powder
140g (5 oz) good-quality dark chocolate sprinkles

1   In a medium, heavy-based saucepan, place the condensed milk, butter, double cream and corn syrup and bring to the boil over a medium heat.

2   When the mixture starts to bubble, add the chocolate and cocoa powder. Whisk well, making sure there are no pockets of cocoa powder. Reduce the heat to low and cook, whisking constantly, until it is dense and fudgy, about 8–10 minutes. You want the mixture to bubble towards the end, so it's important to use a low heat or the side of the pan will burn the fudge. If you undercook it, the *brigadeiro* will be too soft; if you overcook it, it will be too chewy. It is done when you swirl the pan and the mixture slides as one soft piece, leaving a thick, burnt residue on the bottom.

3   Slide the mixture into a bowl (without scraping the bottom) and cool at room temperature. Cover the bowl with clingfilm and chill in the refrigerator for at least 4 hours.

4   Scoop the mixture by the teaspoonful and, using your hands, roll each into a little ball about 2cm (¾ inch) in diameter (about the size of a chocolate truffle).

5   Place the sprinkles in a bowl. Roll 4–6 *brigadeiros* at a time through the sprinkles, making sure they cover the entire surface. Store in an airtight plastic container for 2 days or up to 1 month in the refrigerator. Make sure to eat them at room temperature.

COCONUT BRIGADEIROS

Brigadeiro de Côco

1 395-g (14-oz) can sweetened condensed milk
125ml (4fl oz) coconut milk
2 teaspoons light corn syrup
25g (1 oz) unsalted butter
125g (4½ oz) dessicated coconut

Here's another version that I love and often catch myself sneaking in the kitchen at night to eat another one. Or two. Or six. If you can't find dessicated coconut, buy flaked coconut or coconut chips and shred them in a food processor or grate them on the smallest hole of a grater. Be sure you buy unsweetened coconut, or else this recipe will be much too sweet.

1   In a medium heavy-based saucepan, place the condensed milk, coconut milk, corn syrup, butter and 40g (1½ oz) of the coconut. Bring to the boil over a medium heat.

2   Reduce the heat to low and whisk constantly until the mixture is dense and fudgy, about 8–10 minutes. You want the mixture to bubble, so it's important to use a low heat or else the side of the pan will burn the coconut fudge. You know it is done when you swirl the pan around and the whole mixture slides as one soft piece, leaving burnt residue on the bottom of the pan.

3   Slide the mixture into a bowl (without scraping the bottom) and leave to cool at room temperature. Cover with clingfilm and refrigerate for at least 4 hours.

4   Scoop the mixture by the teaspoonful and, using your hands, roll each into a little ball, 2cm (¾ inch) in diameter.

5   Place the remaining coconut in a bowl. Roll 4–6 *brigadeiros* at a time through the coconut, making sure it sticks and covers the entire outside surfaces. Store in an airtight plastic container at room temperature for 2 days or up to 1 month in the refrigerator. Eat them at room temperature.

ORIGINS OF A NAME:

The name 'brigaderio' comes from a Brazilian political figure, a Brigadier named Eduardo Gomes, who in the early 1900s was admired for his good looks and who notoriously loved chocolate. When sweetened condensed milk was invented (in Switzerland) and brought to Brazil, cooks created this fudge using the sweet milk and chocolate. Legend has it that he liked it so much, the brigadeiro was named in his honour. Today, it is a standard in cafés, snack bars and restaurants all over the country.

PISTACHIO BRIGADEIROS

Brigadeiro de Pistache

As you can tell, it becomes addictive exploring new variations of this popular candy. I love using pistachios for their beautiful colour and nutty taste. Fabri is an Italian brand of pistachio paste available at www.muscofood.com. Like all *brigadeiro* recipes, call all kids in the house to help.

MAKES ABOUT 30 BRIGADERIOS

1 395-g (14-oz) can sweetened condensed milk
3 tablespoons double cream
1 teaspoon light corn syrup
2 tablespoons pistachio paste, preferably Fabri
1 tablespoon unsalted butter
90g (3¼ oz) finely ground pistachios

1   Place the condensed milk, double cream, corn syrup, pistachio paste and butter in a medium saucepan and bring to the boil over a medium heat.

2   As soon as it starts to boil, turn the heat to low and cook, whisking constantly, while the milk thickens into a dense fudge, about 8–10 minutes. You know it is done when you tilt the pan and the whole fudge slides as a piece, leaving the burnt bits on the bottom of the pan.

3   Slide the mixture into a bowl, without scraping the bottom of the pan. Leave to cool at room temperature. Cover the bowl with clingfilm and refrigerate for at least 4 hours.

4   Scoop the mixture by the teaspoonful and, using your hands, roll each into a little ball, 2cm (¾ inch) in diameter.

5   Place the ground pistachios in a bowl. Roll 4–6 *brigadeiros* at a time in the nuts, making sure they cover the entire surface. Store in an airtight plastic container at room temperature for 2 days or up to 1 month in the refrigerator. Eat them at room temperature.

MOLTON DULCE
DE LECHE CAKE

Bolinho Quente de Doce de Leite

Dulce de leche is now available at most supermarkets. Argentinean brands such as San Ignacio and La Salamandra make silky and smooth caramelised milks. However, I used the canned Nestle brand to develop this recipe and was quite happy with the results. The idea to serve this cake alongside soured cream sorbet came from the typical Brazilian pairing of dulce de leche with cheese. The contrast of sweet and tangy, hot and cold, turned this dessert into one of my all time favourites. If you want to serve it with vanilla ice cream it will still be incredible. Try this combination and I guarantee you will devour every bite of it.

SERVES 4

115g (4 oz) butter, plus extra for greasing
300ml (10fl oz) dulce de leche, at room temperature
2 large egg yolks
2 large eggs
2 tablespoons sugar
⅛ teaspoon salt
¼ teaspoon ground cinnamon
1 teaspoon vanilla extract
35g (1 ¼ oz) plain flour, sifted, plus extra for dusting

4 x 175-ml (6-fl oz) foil cake cases or fluted tin cups

SOURED CREAM SORBET

Bring 6fl oz water, 110g sugar, 2 tablespoons light corn syrup and 1 tablespoon of lemon zest to the boil. Strain directly into an ice bath and let cool completely. Whisk in 473ml soured cream. Adjust the taste with 1–2 tablespoons of fresh lemon juice and chill for 6 hours. Run the mixture through an ice-cream machine according to the instructions.

1   Preheat the oven to 180°C/350°F/Gas Mark 4. Using a pastry brush, brush with butter and dust the cases with flour. Shake off the excess flour.

2   Melt the butter in a medium saucepan over a very low heat. When the butter is just melted, remove the pan from the heat and add the dulce de leche. Whisk slowly and constantly until blended, 3–5 minutes.

3   In another bowl, whisk the yolks and whole eggs together. Add the sugar and salt. Pour the dulce de leche mixture into the eggs and whisk well. Add the cinnamon and vanilla and continue to whisk. Add the flour and fold in gently with a rubber spatula, making sure there are no lumps.

4   Carefully pour the mixture into the cases, filling each one almost to the top. (This can be done up to 5 days ahead and left in the refrigerator.) Bake the cakes until the edges are set but the centre is still soft, about 6–8 minutes. (Be aware that the cake will not change much in colour during the baking time, nor will it rise.) Remember each oven is different and this is a delicate recipe. It's more important that you know what to look for than to rely on the exact minute amount.

5   Remove the cakes from the oven. Immediately invert each case onto a plate and serve with sorbet.

AVOCADO CRÈME BRÛLÉE

Crème Brûlée de Abacate

Most people think of only guacamole and salads when it comes to avocado but I really love to use avocados in desserts, the way we do in Brazil. The buttery texture of avocado lends a perfect creaminess to this re-invented crème brûlée which, unlike the classic recipe, is not baked at all. This mixture of avocado and condensed milk is simply puréed in a food processor. After you have simulated the consistency of a custard, you add a crunchy layer of burnt sugar on top immediately before serving. The result is a truly inspired dessert that takes less than 5 minutes to make plus a little chilling time. Because of its richness, this dessert can also act as a mini crème brûlée: simply serve it in smaller ramekins. This will yield more servings, of course, depending on how small a ramekin you use.

FINDING BLOW TORCHES

Because crème brûlée has become so popular, it is very easy to find blowtorches these days. If there are no high-end kitchen stores around you, most DIY stores carry them. However, if you can't find one, you can use a grill. Preheat the grill and place the ramekins in an ice bath in a roasting tin. Spread the sugar as described in the recipe, and place the pan under the grill. Depending on your grill, it can take seconds or minutes to caramelise the sugar, so stand by watching very carefully. When the sugar starts to bubble, remove the roasting tin from the grill, then remove the ramekins from the ice bath.

SERVES 4

300ml (10fl oz) sweetened condensed milk
2 medium firm-ripe Hass avocados, peeled, stoned and cut into chunks
2–3 tablespoons freshly squeezed lemon juice
100g (3½ oz) sugar, for topping

propane blowtorch
4 x 120ml (4fl oz) ramekins

1   Place the condensed milk and avocados in a food processor and process until the mixture is velvety smooth, about 1–2 minutes. Add the lemon juice a tablespoon at a time, and pulse for a few more seconds after each addition. At this point, taste the avocado cream to check if the lemon juice is giving the right balance. I usually use 2 tablespoons and add a drop or two more if necessary.

2   Using a rubber spatula, scrape the mixture into the ramekins, making sure that it is level inside the ramekin. Chill for 4 hours in the refrigerator.

3   Just before serving, spread a thin layer of sugar evenly over the top of each custard. Ignite the blowtorch to medium. Melt the sugar by moving the flame back and forth across the custard while maintaining a distance of 5cm (2 inches) between the flame and the surface. The sugar will melt, bubble, then turn into a golden caramel. In less than a minute, it will harden to a delicious crust. Allow to cool for 3–5 minutes before serving. Do not brûlée the dessert more then 20 minutes in advance of serving.

BRAZILIAN CRÈME CARAMEL

Pudim de Leite

Almost every cuisine has its version of crème caramel, but what makes the Brazilian take so special is the use of sweetened condensed milk, lending a smooth, silky and velvety texture to the dish. In the traditional recipe, only milk is used, but I add a little double cream and extra yolks to expand upon the velvety texture that I like so much. As easy a recipe as crème caramel is, I often see them baked too long or perforated with unsightly holes. With this recipe, the result is an entire spoonful of luxuriously smooth custard, with a caramel sauce oozing its way into every bite. You can prepare the dessert up to 5 days ahead of time and only invert it the day you are serving.

SERVES 6–8

140g (5 oz) sugar

3 tablespoons water

1 x 397g (14-oz) tin sweetened condensed milk

375ml (13fl oz) full-fat milk

125ml (4fl oz) double cream

3 large eggs

2 large egg yolks

1 teaspoon vanilla extract

20 x 5 x 10-cm (8 x 2 x 4-inch) round cake tin or
  4 x 180ml ramekins)

1   Preheat the oven to 180°C/350°F/Gas Mark 4.

2   Place the sugar and water in a heavy-based saucepan. Cook the sugar over a high heat, without stirring, until it turns into an amber-coloured caramel, about 5 minutes. Pour the caramel into the cake tin and swirl around making sure that the caramel evenly covers the whole base. You don't want to have any concentrated lumps of caramel in any part of the tin. Be advised that the caramel will continue to cook once it's off the heat, so work fast. Set the tin aside.

3   Mix all the remaining ingredients in a food processor until smooth. Slowly pour the mixture into the prepared tin. Transfer the tin to a large roasting tin and fill with warm water so that it comes halfway up the side of the cake tin. Place the roasting tin in the centre of the oven and bake until the custard is set, about 45–55 minutes.

5   Cool the tin on a wire rack, then refrigerate for at least 4 hours. It's important to invert the flan only when it is chilled completely, otherwise it might break.

6   When ready to serve, run a smooth knife around the inside of the tin. Place a large rimmed platter on top and, holding the dishes together with both hands, quickly invert the flan onto the platter. Hold for a minute to ensure all the caramel drips onto the platter.

PORTUGUESE-STYLE ALMOND CAKE

Toucinho do Céu

Like many other recipes inherited from Portugal, the origin of *Toucinho do Ceu* goes back hundreds of years to the convents where nuns used to cook sweets based on eggs and sugar and prepare recipes such as *pao de lo* (genoise cake), crème caramel and custards. *Toucinho do Ceu* translates into 'bacon-from-heaven' thanks to the traditional version of this recipe being made with pork lard. This lighter version has as much flavour without the fat. Unlike most almond cakes, which start with a creamy mixture, this cake is prepared by cooking ground almonds in a simple syrup. The result is a very moist almond cake. While this makes a great snack, it's especially good as a dessert when paired with rhubarb and strawberry compote and some sweetened crème fraîche. It can also travel well when made in a bar form, like brownies.

SERVES 6–8

125ml (4fl oz) water
225g (8 oz) sugar
⅛ teaspoon salt
150g (5½ oz) ground almonds
55g (2 oz) unsalted butter, at room temperature, plus extra for greasing
5 large egg yolks
2 large eggs
1 teaspoon almond extract (or Amaretto)
1 teaspoon finely grated orange zest
plain flour, for dusting

20 x 5 x 10-cm (8 x 2 x 4-inch) round cake tin

1   Preheat the oven to 160°C/325°F/Gas Mark 3. Line the cake tin with baking paper. Grease with butter and dust lightly with flour.

2   Bring the water, sugar and salt to the boil in a big saucepan. Add the ground almonds. Stir gently but constantly over a medium-low heat until the mixture starts to thicken and you can see the bottom of the pan by stirring, about 2 minutes. Remove the pan from the heat and add the butter. Mix until the butter is melted and blended well.

3   In a medium bowl, lightly whisk the yolks and whole eggs, then mix into the almond mixture with a spatula. Add the almond extract and orange zest and stir well.

4   Pour the mixture into the prepared tin. Bake until the cake is firm in the centre and the top is lightly golden brown, about 28–30 minutes (if you overbake it, the cake becomes chewy). Cool on a wire rack.

5   Invert the cake onto a platter (see opposite for technique). Lift off the tin, peel off the baking paper and cut the cake into wedges. Serve at room temperature.

COCONUT CUSTARD CAKE

Quindins

The Portuguese deserve all the credit for the love of sweets in Brazil. The African and indigenous heritages contributed more to the ingredients that were incorporated into Portuguese sweets than with the original recipes. For instance, *quindims* were developed by African women to please the Portuguese palates. It is a firm custard made from simple ingredients with an incredibly silky texture resulting from the slow-cooked egg yolks. The lime juice is a crucial ingredient to balance the sweetness. I owe many thanks to Carlos Coelho, the owner of a store that specialises in Brazilian ingredients in Bridgeport, Connecticut. Once, he took me to the kitchen just when the cook was preparing *quindim*. Of all the *quindims* I have tried in my life, this little but complete store in CT offered my favourite version, which is adapted opposite.

SERVES 8–10

14 large egg yolks
1 large egg
200g (7 oz) sugar, plus extra for coating
⅛ teaspoon salt
75ml (2½fl oz) plus 2 tablespoons full-fat milk
70g (2½ oz) unsweetened dessicated coconut
1 teaspoon freshly squeezed lime juice

butter, softened, for greasing
8–10-hole muffin tin

1 Preheat the oven to 160°C/325°F/Gas Mark 3. Butter the sides and bases of each muffin hole and coat the insides with sugar. Shake off the excess and set them aside.

2 In a medium bowl, whisk the yolks, whole egg sugar and salt until they are blended and slightly thickened. Add the milk and whisk well. Add the coconut and lime juice, then fold in everything with a rubber spatula.

3 Pour the mixture into the prepared muffin tin, filling each hole close to the top, but leaving about a 5-mm (¼-inch) space to the edge. Stand the muffin tin inside a roasting tin in the preheated oven. After placing the roasting tin on the oven shelf, pour warm water into the roasting tin under the muffin tin (or you can do this on the work surface,

but just be careful not to let any water drop into the mixture when moving the roasting tin). This process is crucial to give this cake the right texture.

4   Bake until the custard is set and the top is lightly golden brown, about 35–40 minutes. While in the oven, the coconut will rise to the top and create a crust; it can easily become too chewy if overcooked, since it is the only part not receiving protection from the water bath, so remove the roasting tin from the oven as soon as it turns golden brown.

5   Cool the muffin tin on a wire rack for 20–30 minutes.

6   To unmould the *quindims*, run a small paring knife between the pan and each cake; each *quindim* should rotate inside the mould as you run the knife – that's a sign that it is cooked just right. Carefully invert the muffin tin to let all *quindims* out. Give the tin a sharp tap, and the cake should unmould easily. If it doesn't, flip the tin back over and place it over a low burner for just a few seconds to melt the butter under the cakes.

7   Serve slightly chilled. You can prepare the *quindims* up to 5 days ahead of time and keep them in an airtight plastic container in the refrigerator.

GUAVA PASTE SOUFFLÉ WITH MASCARPONE SAUCE

Suflê de Goiabada com Calda de Mascarpone

This dish tells you a lot about what kind of restaurant Carlota is: contemporary Brazilian cooking. Chef and owner, Carla Pernambuco, is one of the most influential chefs in Brazil. One of her classic creations is a *Suflê de Goiabada com Calda de Catupiry*. It's a dish that translates the essence of Brazilian tradition to style and creativity. In my American kitchen, I adapted the recipe using mascarpone instead of Catupiry cheese because it's easier to find and the result is simply fantastic. Unlike most soufflés that deflate within minutes out of the oven, this one is a bit more forgiving, giving you about 10, but like every other soufflé you should whisk the egg whites just before baking. When working with fruit, it is natural to have taste variation due to ripeness, time of harvest and the levels of sugar and pectin in the fruit. Different brands of guava paste, for example, present different consistencies and you might need to adjust with more or less water to dissolve it. When I use the Fugini brand from Brazil, I only need 125ml (4fl oz) water. When I use the Goya brand, I need about 300ml (10fl oz) water.

SERVES 8

FOR THE MASCARPONE SAUCE

1 vanilla pod, scraped (see panel on page 155)
225ml (8fl oz) double cream
1 tablespoon sugar
225ml (8fl oz) mascarpone cheese

550g (1lb 4 oz) guava paste
1 teaspoon freshly squeezed lemon juice
8 egg whites
1/8 teaspoon salt
1½ tablespoons sugar
butter, for greasing, plus extra for coating
icing sugar, for dusting

8 x 180ml (6fl oz) ramekins

---

1   In a medium saucepan, place the double cream, sugar, vanilla pod and its seeds and bring to the boil, whisking well to dissolve the sugar. Reduce the heat to low, add the cheese and whisk slowly, making sure the cheese is melting into the sauce. Remove the vanilla pod and pour the sauce into a serving bowl. This sauce can be prepared up to 3 days ahead of time and kept in an airtight plastic container in the refrigerator. To reheat, warm gently over a low heat and whisk occasionally.

2   Preheat the oven to 180°C/350°F/Gas Mark 4. Grease the ramekins with a thick coat of butter and sprinkle with sugar, tapping out the excess.

3   Cut the guava paste into small chunks and place them in a medium saucepan. Add about 125ml (4fl oz) of water (more or less may be necessary). Cook over a low heat, whisking constantly, until the paste melts. You are looking for a thick and pasty sauce without too much liquid. Remove from the heat.

4   Add the lemon juice and whisk well. Transfer the guava paste to a bowl and let it cool to room temperature, about 20 minutes. This step can be done up to 5 days ahead and the sauce kept in an airtight plastic container in the refrigerator (just make sure you bring it to room temperature before mixing with the egg whites).

5   Working in a clean, dry bowl of an electric mixer fitted with the whisk attachment, whisk the egg whites with the salt until they just turn opaque, gradually increasing the speed from medium to high.

6   Still beating, add the sugar in a slow, steady stream and continue to beat until the peaks are firm and shiny. Using a large rubber spatula, fold one-quarter of the egg whites into the guava paste. Gently fold in the remaining egg whites, making sure that the batter is well folded, without any lumps.

7   Delicately turn the mixture into the prepared ramekins. I like to use a piping bag without a tip for this task, but a plain ladle will also work. Fill the ramekins almost to the top and place on a baking sheet. Bake the soufflés in the oven until the tops become lightly brown, about 12 minutes.

8   Remove the soufflés from the oven and dust them with icing sugar. To serve, poke a hole in the centre of each soufflé and pour some sauce inside.

PASSION FRUIT CANNOLI

Cannoli de Maracujá

Cannoli is one of my favourite Italian pastries. The classic Italian version has a crisp, tubular shell filled with a creamy ricotta flavoured with crystallised fruit. The Americanised version using chocolate chips has already become the new classic. Instead of using milk, I use coconut milk and passion fruit to lend a delicious mix of exotic and tropical flavours. These are not the easiest tuilles to work with because they harden quite fast. You have to spread it thin enough for a delicate cannoli, but not so thin that it breaks. Another option for presentation is to keep the tuilles flat and build a napoleon as opposed to a cannoli. Either way, this dessert is quite easy to do at home because everything is prepared ahead of time. But assembling must be done just before serving. If you want to get a little fancy, garnish wth some fresh berries and a coriander syrup (see panel opposite).

FOR THE PASTRY CREAM

325ml (11fl oz) coconut milk
75ml (2½fl oz) passion fruit juice, from concentrate
60g (2¼ oz) sugar
35g (1 oz)
6 large egg yolks

FOR THE TUILLES

115g (4 oz) toasted almonds
25g (1 oz) unsweetened dessicated coconut
1 tablespoon plain four
1 tablespoon cocoa powder
2 tablespoons coconut milk
2 tablespoons light corn syrup
50g (1¾ oz) sugar
70g (2½ oz) unsalted butter

6–8 cannoli tubes

1 Make the pastry cream. In a medium saucepan, bring the coconut milk and passion fruit juice to a boil over a medium heat.

2 In a bowl, whisk together the egg yolks and sugar. Add the cornflour and whisk until blended. Whisking all the while, pour about a quarter of the hot liquid into the yolk mixture. Still whisking, add the remaining hot liquid to the yolks. Whisk well and transfer this mixture back to the saucepan.

3 Place the saucepan over a medium-low heat and cook, whisking vigorously, until the cream starts to thicken turns from liquid into a creamy consistency, about 5 minutes.

4 Cover a baking tray with a layer of clingfilm and pour the cream onto it. Spread into a thin

5   layer and cool to room temperature. Cover with clingfilm and refrigerate for at least 2 hours or up to 2 days.

5   Meanwhile, make the tuilles. In the bowl of a food processor, grind the almonds and coconut until they become a fine powder, about 1 minute. Add the flour and cocoa powder and process until it's well blended. Transfer to a bowl and set aside.

6   In a medium saucepan, bring the coconut milk, corn syrup, sugar and butter to the boil. Reduce the heat to low and cook until the mixture bubbles vigorously, about 3 minutes. Remove the pan from the heat and add the almond-coconut mixture. Fold together with a rubber spatula until well blended.

7   At this point you have to work relatively fast or else the mixture might harden. Split the mixture in half and spread each half onto a 30 x 46-cm (12 x 18-inch) baking sheet lined with baking paper. Cover each sheet with another sheet of baking paper. Using a rolling pin, roll into a thin layer, spreading the mixture to fit the sheet. Chill in the refrigerator until the tuiles harden, about 2 hours.

8   Preheat the oven to 180°C/350°F/Gas Mark 4. Remove the tuilles from the refrigerator. Using a 7.5-cm (3-inch) round pastry cutter, cut 10–12 rounds of tuile per baking sheet. Line a baking sheet with baking paper and place 6 tuilles on it, leaving at least 7.5 cm (3 inches) between each tuille. (You can store sheets of baking paper lined with rounds of tuille in the refrigerator for up to 5 days or in the freezer for up to a month.)

9   Bake the tuilles in the oven until they bubble and look done, about 8 minutes. Immediately remove the baking sheet from the oven and, using a flat offset spatula, flip each round upside down so that the textured side faces up. Roll around a cannoli tube (don't roll it too tight or it may be difficult to remove the metal tube from inside the tuille), being careful not to burn your fingers. Let each rolled tuille harden around the cannoli tube for at least 2 minutes to maintain its round shape before pushing the tube out. If while you are rolling some tuilles other become hard, reheat them in the oven for another minute before rolling. Repeat the process with all the mixture.

10   Remove the cream from the refrigerator at least 30 minutes before assembling. Beat in the bowl of an electric mixer fitted with the paddle attachment at medium speed to lighten up the cream. Place the pastry cream in a piping bag or zip-lock plastic bag. Cut a small opening and carefully pipe into both ends of the cannoli.

MAKING SYRUP

When I was working in restaurant pastry kitchens, I learnt that chefs like to keep some herb-syrups (such as coriander, mint or basil) to use as garnishes. It's quite easy to make one: plunge a good handful of herbs into boiling water for 15 seconds, drain and plunge into an iced water bath. Remove the herbs from the water and combine them in a blender or food processor with 225g (8 oz) light corn syrup. Blend, strain and discard the solids. The syrup will keep fresh, covered in the refrigerator, for 1–2 days.

COFFEE SOUFFLÉ WITH DULCE DE LECHE SAUCE

Suflê de Café com Calda de Doce de Leite

Coffee is one of Brazil's most important commodities and I was itching to make a dessert using such a traditional Brazilian flavour. I tried it in mousses, custards and parfaits. But there is something about a hot soufflé that brings you closer to the sensation of drinking a cup of strong, freshly brewed coffee. The sweetness of the dulce de leche sauce complements the flavour of coffee and adds a velvety taste to the airy texture of a soufflé.

SERVES 6

350ml (12fl oz) milk
4 teaspoons instant espresso coffee powder
5 large egg yolks
60g (2¼ oz) sugar
16g (½ oz) plain flour
16g (½ oz) cornflour

8 egg whites
pinch of salt
3 tablespoons sugar
icing sugar, for dusting
Dulce de Leche Sauce (see opposite)

6 x 175-ml (6fl oz) ramekins, greased

1 Preheat the oven to 180°C/350°F/Gas Mark 4. In a medium saucepan, bring the milk to a boil. Turn off the heat and whisk in the instant coffee.

2 In a separate bowl, whisk together the egg yolks with the sugar until yellow and pale.

3 Sift together the flour and cornflour and add to the egg yolks, whisking until there are no lumps. Carefully pour in the hot milk, always whisking well. Transfer back to the saucepan and cook over a low heat, whisking constantly, until it thickens, about 4 minutes. Transfer to a bowl and leave to cool.

4 In the bowl of an electric mixer fitted with the whisk attachment, beat the egg whites with the salt until they foam and rise. Gradually add the sugar and beat at medium-high speed until glossy soft peaks form.

5 Using a large spatula, fold one-quarter of the whites into the pastry cream to lighten it, then gently fold in the remaining whites. Pour the soufflé mixture into the ramekins to three-quarters. Place on a baking sheet and bake until they are puffed and golden brown, about 15–18 minutes.

6 Remove from the oven and dust with icing sugar. Poke a hole in the centre of each soufflé and pour in some warm Dulce de Leche Sauce. Serve immediately.

HOT DULCE DE LECHE SAUCE

Calda de Doce de Leite

This recipe is incredibly easy to make and serves many purposes. I like to use it not only as a sauce for soufflés but also for ice cream toppings, in crêpes and with many other desserts. It is versatile: spreadable when cold and pourable when warm.

MAKES 475ML (17FL OZ)

225ml (8fl oz) milk
125ml (4fl oz) double cream
25g (1 oz) unsalted butter
300ml (10fl oz) dulce de leche (see page 137),
    at room temperature

1 In a heavy-based saucepan, combine the milk, double cream and butter and bring to the boil over a high heat. Boil for 1 minute and remove the pan from the heat.

2 Add the dulce de leche and whisk gently but constantly in ever-widening circles.

3 When smooth, return the saucepan to the hob and cook over a high heat, whisking constantly, until you reach a full boil. Reduce the heat to medium and cook, still whisking, until the sauce becomes thick and creamy, about 3–5 minutes.

4 If you want to use the sauce in its pourable state, let it cool for about 10 minutes. If you want to save it for later, keep it in a plastic container covered with a tight-fitting lid for at least 2 weeks in the refrigerator (reheat in a saucepan over a low heat, whisking constantly, or in the microwave, 10 seconds at a time, whisking after each turn, until it's hot and pourable).

FIG TERRINE WITH DULCE DE LECHE SAUCE

Terrine de Figos com Calda de Doce de Leite e Avelãs

This dessert is based on a method I learnt from a caterer in Rio when I was 15. Demar is known for his perfect fig desserts, and when I asked him how he prepared them, he explained that when figs are peeled and packed together, they stick to each other as if they are one large fruit. I have been using that little trick for years. Here, I use a loaf tin, so I had to use lots and lots of figs to fill it up. But you can use any size mould you have or even a small round cake tin, as long as you pack it full. The pairing of the cold moulded fruit with the warm Dulce de Leche Sauce makes this dessert a decadent experience of taste, temperature and texture – not to mention a beautiful presentation. Unmoulding this terrine is a glorious unveiling that should be done in front of your guests. Garnish with toasted and chopped hazelnuts for crunch.

SERVES 8

1.1kg (2lb 8 oz) fresh figs, about 40
Dulce de Leche Sauce (see page 149)

23 x 7.5 x 7.5-cm (9 x 3 x 3-inch) loaf tin

BUYING FIGS

There are three types of figs: Black Mission, kadota and Brown Turkey. Any kind can be used for this recipe because the difference in taste is very slim. However, don't mix the varieties because the colour of the terrine will be unharmonious. Figs are quite perishable, so I would recommend preparing the terrine not more than 1 or 2 days before serving. Try to choose figs that are not too green or too ripe. If you press the fruit with your thumb, it should feel slightly soft.

1 Line the loaf tin with clingfilm, making sure the plastic is touching the walls and the bottom of the tin (spritz the tin with a little water to help the clingfilm stick to it). Use more than enough clingfilm to line the tin as you'll need excess to then seal the top of it after the figs are packed in.

2 Cut off the top stems, then peel and cut all the figs in half. Arrange the figs inside the tin, with their centres facing out, lightly pressing them together and making sure there is minimal space between each fig. Seal the tin with the extra clingfilm and place it, open-side up, in the refrigerator to chill overnight.

3 When it is time to serve, open the clingfilm, place the terrine facing down on a rectangular plate or a chopping board and lift off the loaf tin. Peel off the clingfilm. Using a serrated knife, cut slices about 2.5 cm (1 inch) thick and place each one on a plate. The slices on the ends won't look as pretty and won't hold as well as the rest of the slices in the centre. Remember that there is nothing holding the figs together other than Mother Nature, so make sure you aim for a 2.5-cm (1-inch) thickness or the figs will fall apart.

4 Pour warm Dulce de Leche Sauce on top of each slice.

CHURROS

This recipe is based on the churros I often eat at Praca Nossa Senhora da Paz, in Ipanema. They are sold in carts that cluster the corners of Rio's streets; on weekends, they relocate to the vast stretches of our Atlantic beaches. Served in a small paper bag, you get crispy fried dough, dusted with cinnamon sugar, and filled from top to bottom with an injection of dulce de leche squirting out from the centre and dripping onto your fingers. Unlike an American doughnut, the centre remains pale, moist, and chewy.

In looking to adapt this indulgent experience for our home kitchens, I bought the largest star nozzle I could find (about 2.5cm/1 inch in diameter on the opening), two piping bags (one for the dough, one for the dulce de leche) and a tube nozzle (a piping bag nozzle that has a thin 5-cm/2-inch tube attached). The size of the star nozzle is key to the success of churros – if it's not wide enough, the churros will be too thin and much too crunchy.

200g (7 oz) sugar, plus 1 teaspoon

1 tablespoon ground cinnamon

140g (5 oz) plain flour, plus extra for dusting

1 teaspoon baking powder

350ml (12fl oz) water

1 tablespoon olive oil

⅛ teaspoon salt

2 litres vegetable oil, for deep-frying

1 x 397-g (14-oz) tin dulce de leche, at
   room temperature

ORIGINS OF CHURROS

Many churros recipes are based on a choux dough served with a chocolate sauce. For such an admitted chocoholic like me, it's surprisingly abnormal to feel this way but I don't think churros and chocolate make a good match. In my opinion, the flavour of chocolate overwhelms the fried dough and the consistency of the sauce is too thin. In Brazil, we serve it filled with dulce de leche. The dough is also different, based on flour and water only, no eggs at all; it is stiff enough to be shaped, but also moist enough to retain some sponginess.

1   In a shallow bowl, combine the 200g (7 oz) sugar and cinnamon and mix well. Set aside.

2   In a small bowl, sift together the flour and baking powder.

3   In a medium saucepan, bring the water, olive oil, salt and teaspoon sugar to the boil. Add the flour all at once and mix vigorously until a dough forms and pulls away from the side of the pan, about 30 seconds. The dough will look stiff and not very smooth.

4   Transfer the dough to a floured surface and let cool, about 10 minutes. Knead the dough lightly with your hands until it becomes a smooth ball.

5   Fill a medium saucepan with 5cm (2 inches) of oil. Heat the oil to 180°C/350°F, as measured by a deep-fat frying thermometer.

6   Spoon the dough into a piping bag fitted with the largest star nozzle you can find. Hold the piping bag directly above the oil and squeeze in strips of dough about 4–5 inches long, snipping them with your finger. Fry them in

batches until lightly golden brown all over, about 2–3 minutes.

7   Using a slotted spoon, transfer the churros to a flat plate lined with a double thickness of kitchen paper to absorb any excess oil. Let the churros dry for a minute and, while still hot, roll them in the cinnamon sugar mixture. (Churros can be cooked in advance and kept warm in a low temperature oven).

8   Spoon the dulce de leche inside another piping bag fitted with a tube nozzle and insert the tube in the centre of each churro as far as it will go. Apply pressure to release the dulce de leche while slowly moving the tube nozzle out.

9   Serve with plenty of napkins.

COCONUT MOUSSE
Mousse de côco

This classic Brazilian mousse is all about coconut. I like to serve it with a complementary sauce also based on coconut – *Baba de Moça* (see recipe). Cloudy and airy, each bite is rich and refreshing with traces of coconut melting in your mouth. Fresh coconut shavings make the best garnish, but lightly toasted dried coconut chips are just as wonderful. This mousse can be prepared up to 3 days ahead of time and kept in the refrigerator covered with clingfilm.

SERVES 8

1 x 395-g (14-oz) can sweetened condensed milk
400ml (14fl oz) coconut milk
90g (3¼ oz) dessicated or finely grated coconut
2½ teaspoons (1 envelope) unflavoured gelatine
125ml (4fl oz) double cream
4 egg whites
tiny pinch of salt
1 tablespoon sugar
coconut shavings, lightly toasted, to decorate
Coconut Custard Sauce (see opposite), to serve

1. In a medium bowl, whisk together the sweetened condensed milk, 225ml (8fl oz) of the coconut milk and the coconut. Set aside.

2. In a small saucepan, place the remaining coconut milk, sprinkle the gelatine on top and give it a quick whisk. Leave to stand at room temperature for about 2 minutes. Bring to a bare simmer over a very low heat, whisking gently, until the gelatine is dissolved (but do not let it boil), about 1 minute.

3. Pour the gelatine-coconut milk into the sweetened condensed mixture and whisk well. Leave to stand sit at room temperature for 10 minutes.

4. In the bowl of an electric mixer fitted with the whisk attachment, whip the double cream until it holds soft peaks and then gently fold it into the coconut mixture. If you see any lumps, mix with a spatula to get rid of them.

5. In another clean bowl of an electric mixer fitted with the whisk attachment, beat the egg whites with the salt. Start on low speed and gradually increase as the whites begin to foam and rise. Slowly add the sugar and beat until soft peaks form. Fold it gently into the coconut mixture, knowing that, just like the whipped cream, the egg whites will become somewhat liquid once they are mixed into the base. Make sure there are no lumps.

6. Pour the coconut mousse into a nice glass bowl and cover with clingfilm. Chill in the refrigerator until it's set, about 6 hours, preferably overnight.

7. To serve, decorate with some toasted coconut shavings and Coconut Custard Sauce.

COCONUT CUSTARD SAUCE

Baba de Moça

<table>
<tr><td>MAKES 475ML (17FL OZ)</td></tr>
</table>

400ml (14fl oz) coconut milk
80ml (2½fl oz) full-fat milk
1 vanilla pod
6 large egg yolks
115g (4 oz) sugar

Based on egg yolks, coconut milk and sugar, this classic sauce, when served by itself, was among my favourite childhood treats. Like a crème Anglaise, *Baba de Moça* is a very versatile sauce – I serve it with coconut mousse, chocolate cake and many other desserts. I hope you will find many uses for this recipe, but don't feel guilty sampling it straight from the spoon.

1   In a medium saucepan, bring the milk, coconut milk and scraped vanilla pod to the boil.

2   In a bowl, whisk together the egg yolks and sugar until the mixture becomes thick and pale yellow. Drizzle a little of the hot milk into the yolks to prevent them from curdling, then slowly pour in the remaining milk, whisking vigorously all the while.

3   Return the sauce to the saucepan and cook over a low heat, stirring with a wooden spoon, until the custard thickens and coats the back of the spoon.

4   Immediately remove the pan from the heat and strain the custard through a fine sieve into a bowl. Discard the vanilla pod and place the bowl over an ice bath. When it is chilled, place the sauce in a plastic container, cover with a tight-fitting lid and store it in the refrigerator. This sauce can be prepared up to 3 days ahead of serving.

VANILLA PODS

The best vanilla pods come from Madagascar, Tahiti and Mexico. When buying vanilla pods, make sure they are soft and oily, not dry. A good vanilla pod should bend, not crack, when split in half. If it cracks, don't even bother using it because the bean is old and dry and the flavour is almost gone. Always store vanilla pods wrapped in a zip-lock plastic bag in a dry place, like a pantry. Do not store vanilla pods in the refrigerator. To scrape a vanilla bean, slice it in half lengthways with a sharp knife and use the blunt side of the knife to scrape out the pulp. Add both the pulp and the pod to the recipe. Many pastry chefs infuse their sugar with vanilla pods. To do so, simply air-dry a vanilla pod after use, then bury it in white granulated sugar and store it in an airtight jar. This is an easy way to add extra flavour to all of your desserts.

CHOCOLATE AND CUPUAÇU PUDDING

Copa de Chocolate e Cupuaçu

The scent of *cupuaçu* recalls the exotic perfumes of the Amazon. *Cupuaçu's* taste is quite hard to describe, but it falls somewhere between a banana and white chocolate, with an alcoholic tang at the end. It's a delicious reward for an exploratory palate. It's not hard to harness this unknown fruit into a delectable dessert. Simply make a pastry cream and add the fruit pulp at the end, then make a chocolate ganache to pour on top. It tastes like nothing you've ever tried before and it can be assembled up to 5 days before serving.

FOR THE CHOCOLATE CRUMBLE

40g (1½ oz) plain flour

1 tablespoon cornflour

2 tablespoons cocoa powder

35g (1¼ oz) almond flour

⅛ teaspoon salt

50g (1¾ oz) plus 2 tablespoons sugar

55g (2 oz) unsalted butter, at room temperature

FOR THE CUPUAÇU CREAM

250ml (8¾fl oz) full-fat milk

3 large egg yolks

80g (3 oz) sugar

1 tablespoon plain flour, sifted

16g (½ oz) cornflour, sifted

140g (5 oz) cupuaçu pulp, thawed

FOR THE CHOCOLATE GANACHE

225g (8 oz) dark chocolate

300ml (10fl oz) double cream

8 wine glasses or glass ramekins

1 Preheat the oven to 180°C/350°F/Gas Mark 4.

2 In the bowl of an electric mixer fitted with the paddle attachment, mix all the chocolate crumble ingredients together until it resembles a coarse meal. Spread the mixture onto a baking sheet and bake until it is dry, about 12–14 minutes, rotating once. Remove from the oven and leave to cool. (You can prepare this up to 2 days ahead of time and keep it in an airtight plastic container at a cool and dry room temperature.)

3 Meanwhile, prepare the cupuaçu cream. In a medium saucepan, heat the milk over a medium heat.

4 In a medium bowl, whisk together the egg yolks and sugar until they become pale and yellow. Add the flour and cornflour and whisk until blended and thick.

5 Gently drizzle some of the hot milk into the egg yolks to prevent curdling, then add the remaining milk. Transfer the mixture back to the saucepan and cook over a very low heat, whisking constantly (make sure you reach into the edge of the pan), until it takes on a custard's consistency, about 5–7 minutes. Immediately scrape the mixture into a bowl and, while it's still hot, whisk in the cupuaçú pulp. Cool at room temperature, stirring occasionally with a spatula.

6 Fill each glass with about 75ml (2½fl oz) of the cupuaçu cream. Chill in the refrigerator for at least 4 hours. Meanwhile, prepare the chocolate ganache. Chop the chocolate into small pieces and place it in a stainless steel bowl.

7 In a small saucepan, bring the double cream to the boil and immediately pour it over the chocolate. Stir the mixture carefully with a rubber spatula, starting from the centre of the bowl and gradually incorporating the whole mixture until it's only just blended. Leave to cool at room temperature for 20–30 minutes, stirring occasionally with a spatula.

8 Transfer the ganache to a disposable piping bag or zip-lock plastic bag with the corner cut off. Carefully squeeze the chocolate ganache over the cupuaçú cream and tap the side of the glasses to make sure there are no pockets of air. Chill the glasses in the refrigerator for 3 hours or overnight.

9 Remove them from the refrigerator 30 minutes before serving. Decorate with the crumble.

COCONUT CHEESECAKE WITH GUAVA SAUCE

Cheesecake de Côco com Calda de Goiaba

GRATING COCONUT

The most practical form to buy coconut is dessicated and unsweetened. If, however, you prefer to use a fresh coconut, you will need a hammer and a screwdriver to crack it open. Break it up into chunks and peel off the brown skin from the coconut meat. Grate it finely for the crust and shave it more coarsely for the garnish. If the coconut you buy is not fine enough, just pass it through the food processor. You can also toast the coconut shavings. When you shave them, know that bigger is better. Place them in a 150°C/300°F/ Gas Mark 2 oven until they start to become lightly golden brown, about 3–5 minutes.

This is a Brazilian take on a classic American dessert. I changed the regular digestive biscuit crust to a chocolate one (simply process the biscuits in the food processor until they're a fine crumble) and added coconut. It's very important to use unsweetened coconut, otherwise the crust will be sticky. The filling is a combination of Brazilian and American ingredients. It's deliciously creamy and sets up quite well in the presence of gelatine. The guava sauce complements the cheesecake in a classic Brazilian way, while still remaining somewhat close in flavour to the strawberry or cherry sauces often used in the States. I used the guava juice in concentrated form, but you can also use frozen guava pulp by omitting the cornflour and cooking the pulp and sugar together until it thickens slightly.

FOR THE CRUST

140g (5 oz) chocolate digestive biscuit crumbs

35g (1¼ oz) unsweetened finely grated coconut

1 teaspoon sugar

85g (3 oz) unsalted butter, melted and cooled

FOR THE FILLING

2 teaspoons unflavoured powdered gelatine

175ml (6fl oz) coconut milk

115g (4 oz) cream cheese, softened

150ml (5fl oz) condensed milk

125ml (4fl oz) cream

125ml (4fl oz) soured cream

1 tablespoon sugar

1 tablespoon Malibu

50g (1¾ oz) unsweetened grated coconut

FOR THE GUAVA SAUCE

1 tablespoon cornflour

475ml (17fl oz) guava juice, from concentrate

140g (5 oz) sugar

a few drops of freshly squeezed lemon juice, to taste

coconut shavings, lightly toasted

25-cm (10-inch) fluted flan tin or springform cake tin

1   Preheat the oven to 180°C/350°F/Gas Mark 4.

2   For the crust, in the bowl of a food processor or a mixer fitted with the paddle attachment, combine the biscuit crumbs, coconut and sugar. Process until well combined, then slowly drizzle in the butter until the crumbs are uniformly moist. Using your hands, press the mixture into the tin, patting into an even layer on the base and all the way up the side. Bake for 10–12 minutes, then cool on a wire rack.

3   Meanwhile, prepare the filling. In a small saucepan, sprinkle the gelatine over the coconut milk and give it a whisk. Allow the gelatine to soften for 5 minutes.

4   In another medium saucepan, bring the cream cheese and condensed milk to a light simmer over a medium heat. Whisk until smooth, then transfer to a bowl.

5   Over a low heat, bring the gelatine and coconut milk to a low simmer, just until the gelatine melts. Do not let it boil. Immediately pour into the cream cheese mixture, whisk well and let everything cool to room temperature.

6   In the bowl of an electric mixer fitted with the whisk attachment, whip the double cream and soured cream together. Gradually add the sugar and beat until the mixture forms medium peaks. Gently fold the whipped cream with a rubber spatula into the cream cheese mixture. Add the rum and the coconut while folding. Pour the filling into the cooled crust and refrigerate until set, about 4 hours.

7   Meanwhile, prepare the guava sauce. In a small bowl, whisk the cornflour with 3 tablespoons of the guava juice and set aside.

8   In a medium, heavy-based saucepan, bring the remaining guava juice and sugar to a simmer, whisking until hot. Add the cornflour mixture and bring everything to the boil, whisking constantly, until the sauce has thickened to a syrup. Add the lemon juice to taste. Transfer to an airtight container and chill in the refrigerator. (The sauce can be prepared up to 3 days in advance.)

9   Remove the cheesecake from the refrigerator 20–30 minutes before serving. Decorate with toasted coconut shavings and serve with the guava sauce drizzled on top.

PASSION FRUIT CRÊPES SOUFFLÉ

Crepe Suflê de Maracujá

Claude Troisgrois came to Rio in 1978. His father, Pierre, and his uncle, Jean, two of the most famous members of a generation of chefs who defined French cuisine, sealed the Troisgrois name. Claude brought to Rio all the honours of their legacy. He was a pioneer in working with Brazilian ingredients, a movement he created over 30 years ago, and has been inspiring not only a new generation of Brazilian chefs but a new generation of discerning diners to care about their own Brazilian ingredients. The components of this dessert are plain as can be. It's the way they are constructed that makes this recipe so special. The crêpe is a crêpe soufflé: the batter is suspended with egg whites and the crêpe is cooked on one side only, in a pan, then baked in the oven until the edges are set. When it comes out of the oven, it is filled with a small amount of pastry cream. The crêpe is then burnt like a crème brûlée. However, it is very easy to burn – it's worth trying but icing sugar can do the trick as well. This recipe can be done up to 5 days in advance and reheated before serving.

SERVES 10–12

FOR THE SAUCE
100g (3½ oz) sugar
2 tablespoons water
225g (9 oz) passion fruit pulp, thawed
115g (4 oz) unsalted butter, chilled and
    cut into cubes

FOR THE CRÊPES
225ml (8fl oz) full-fat milk
42g (1½ oz) butter, plus extra for cooking the crêpes
5 eggs, separated
100g (3½ oz) sugar, plus extra for sprinkling
65g (2 oz) plain flour, sifted
pinch of salt

FOR THE PASTRY CREAM
See page 146

1   In a medium saucepan, cook the sugar and water over a high heat until the sugar turns a light caramel colour, about 3–5 minutes. (You don't want a dark caramel for this sauce, or it will make the passion fruit sauce bitter.) Add the fruit pulp and cook, whisking constantly, over a low heat for 3–5 minutes. Strain through a fine sieve and pour into another saucepan.

2   Place the saucepan over a very low heat and add the cold pieces of butter, swirling the pan until all the butter has melted. Don't let it boil. This sauce can be made up to

5 days ahead of time; store it in a plastic container covered with a tight fitting lid in the refrigerator.

3   Meanwhile, prepare the crêpes. Preheat the oven to 190°C/375°F/Gas Mark 5.

4   In a medium saucepan, bring the milk and butter to a gentle simmer over a low heat.

5   In the bowl of an electric mixer fitted with the whisk attachment, mix the egg yolks and half of the sugar. Beat until the yolks turn yellow and pale, about 3 minutes. Turn the machine off and add the flour, whisking well by hand until blended.

6   Carefully pour some of the hot milk into the egg yolk mixture, then add the remaining milk. Whisk well by hand. At this point the batter should look creamy. Leave to cool at room temperature for at least 10 minutes.

7   In another bowl of an electric mixer fitted with the whisk attachment, place the egg whites with the salt and beat until they start to foam and rise. Gradually add the remaining sugar, turn the speed to medium-high and beat until glossy soft peaks forms. Using a rubber spatula, fold one-quarter of the egg whites into the yolk mixture, then gently fold in the remaining whites.

8   Heat an omelette pan over a very low heat and melt a knob of butter. Using a medium ladle (175–225ml/6–8fl oz), transfer one ladle of the crêpe batter to the pan and, using the back of the ladle, lightly spread the batter just to the rim of the pan – not up the side. Cook the crêpe over a very low heat for 1–3 minutes. Check the underside of the crêpe by carefully lifting one side of the crêpe. It should look nicely golden brown.

9   Immediately transfer the crêpe to the oven for 3–5 minutes until the edge of the crêpe is very lightly golden brown (if your crêpe pan is not ovenproof, simply slide the crêpe onto a baking sheet and place it in the oven). Don't let the centre of the crêpe become brown.

10   Slide the crêpe onto the work surface and, while still hot (otherwise it won't seal), fill the crêpe with 2 tablespoons of the filling and seal it by pinching the 2 edges tightly with your fingers. It should have the shape of a half moon and be puffed up in the centre.

11   Repeat with all the crêpe batter, making sure to wipe the omelet pan with kitchen paper between each crêpe. As each crêpe is baked, filled and closed, transfer them to a wire rack. You should have enough to make about 10–12 crêpes. This step can be done up to 5 days ahead and kept in a plastic container covered with a tight-fitting lid in the refrigerator.

12   To serve, place all the crêpes on a baking sheet and heat them in a 180°C/350°F/Gas Mark 4 oven for 5 minutes. Gently warm the sauce over a low heat, without letting it boil.

13   Remove the baking sheet from the oven and sprinkle a thin layer of sugar on each crêpe, concentrating on the small, flattest area of the rounded crêpe. Use a blowtorch to burn it, just as if you were burning a crème brûlée (see page 139). You want to caramelise just the sugar, not the crêpe dough.

14   Spoon the sauce equally onto individual plates and swirl to fit the circular shape of the plate. Transfer the caramelised crêpe soufflé to the plate and serve immediately.

PEANUT BRITTLE

Pé de Moleque

Although you can use a variety of nuts, the brittle of my childhood is made with peanuts that are transformed into a munchy-crunchy caramel candy through the addition of sugar, butter, corn syrup, and honey (I learnt from master chef Jacques Torres that honey adds a great touch to brittles). This is culinary alchemy at its best. I love to give brittle as a homemade gift. It can be eaten as a confection on its own or added as a crunchy element to ice cream. When making these sweets, keep in mind that humidity will turn them sticky. The brittle keeps nice and crunchy in a cool and dry place. Be sure to keep the nuts halved or whole, not chopped.

MAKES ABOUT 675G (1LB 8 OZ)

140g (5 oz) sugar
175g (6 oz) unsalted butter
1 teaspoon sea salt
85g (3 oz) light corn syrup
85g (3 oz) honey
395g (14 oz) whole unsalted roasted peanuts

1 In a large, heavy-based saucepan, place the sugar, butter, salt, corn syrup and honey and melt over a medium heat, stirring slowly with a wooden spoon, for 2–3 minutes. As soon as the mixture reaches a pale yellow, add the peanuts and turn the heat to low.

2 Stirring constantly with a wooden spoon, roast the peanuts slowly until they start to turn a golden caramel colour, about 12–15 minutes. You know it's done when the peanuts start to smoke and you lift up the wooden spoon and they hold onto each other (as opposed to falling immediately off the spoon). Be aware that they continue to darken off the heat.

3 Immediately pour the mixture onto a baking sheet lined with baking paper. Cover with another layer of baking paper and use a rolling pin to spread the brittle thinly, trying to fit the baking sheet as best as you can. Be careful not to burn your hands – you have to do this while it's very hot. Let the brittle cool completely at room temperature, then using your hands, break it into 5-cm (2-inch) pieces. Store in an airtight plastic container in a cool and dry place for up to 3 weeks.

PEANUT BUTTER TRUFFLES

Trufas de Paçoca

Paçoca is our version of peanut butter, though it is not puréed and spreadable; rather, the peanuts are ground with a little bit of manioc starch and sugar, then pressed, shaped and wrapped as a sweet. Americans and Brazilians both share not only a love for peanut treats but an affinity for adding chocolate to the mix. You can find *paçoca* in any Brazilian food store or from a supplier, but finely chopped peanuts (with no skin) make a good substitute. If using peanut butter where the butter and the oil have separated, do not mix the oil back; simply pour it out and measure just the paste. When making this recipe, be sure to pay attention to one important detail: temperature (see panel opposite). It affects both the filling and the chocolate coating. When forming the filling, the full batch can become too warm to hold a shape before you finish. To solve this problem, divide the mixture into two batches before you chill it and work with one at a time. If there is one way to make this recipe easier, it is to use top-quality chocolate, such as Valrhona, Guittard, Scharffen Berger, Callebaut or Michel Cluizel, because they all have a great amount of cocoa butter, which is key to tempering chocolate.

200g (7 oz) milk chocolate, chopped

225g (8 oz) crunchy peanut butter

2 tablespoons sugar

1 teaspoon sea salt

40g (1½ oz) unsalted butter, at room temperature

12 paçocas or 280g (10 oz) roasted unsalted peanuts, finely chopped

225g (8 oz) dark chocolate (60–70 per cent cocoa solids), chopped

1   Place the milk chocolate in a stainless steel bowl and set it over a saucepan of simmering water. Make sure the base of the bowl doesn't touch the water. Melt the chocolate, stirring constantly with a rubber spatula. Before the chocolate is all melted, remove the bowl from the heat and stir it as it finishes melting – this prevents the chocolate from overheating. Let it cool without allowing it to harden, about 15 minutes.

2   While the chocolate is cooling, place the peanut butter, sugar and salt in the bowl of a food processor. Process for 3–5 minutes, making sure that the sugar and salt are all dissolved in the peanut butter. Add the cooled chocolate and process until everything is well mixed. Add the butter and continue to process until the butter is all melted, about 2 more minutes.

TEMPERING CHOCOLATE

When making chocolate sweets, it's important to temper the chocolate. When you melt chocolate, you modify the molecules of fat, and in order to make your chocolate nice and shiny again, you need to put the molecules of fat back together the right way – by tempering, or your chocolate will look grainy and stained. My favourite method of tempering chocolate is to add chopped chocolate to the melted chocolate. Many times chocolate is tempered the right way but still measures 33.3–33.9°C/92–93°F on a sugar thermometer. This means I have to wait a few more minutes until the temperature drops just a few more degrees (see below). On the other hand, letting the chocolate sit until it reaches the ideal working temperature is not the best way to do it because the fact that your chocolate is at the right temperature does not mean it was tempered the right way.

Without focusing on any brand, here are the ideal working temperatures for:

Dark chocolate, 31–32.8°C (88–91°F)

Milk Chocolate, 28.9–30°C (84–86°F)

White Chocolate, 27.8–28.9°C (82–84°F)

3 Transfer the mixture equally to 2 plastic containers. Leave to cool to room temperature, then cover with a tight-fitting lid and place in the refrigerator for at least 6 hours, preferably overnight. (The filling can be kept in the refrigerator for up to 2 weeks.)

4 Using a teaspoon, make little balls using the palm of your hands and place them on a flat baking sheet lined with baking paper. Clean your hands often and work with half a batch at a time, keeping the other half cold in the refrigerator. Chill the balls in the refrigerator until set, about 30 minutes. Remove them from the refrigerator about 5 minutes before dipping them in the melted chocolate to avoid a shock of temperatures.

5 To make the coating, crumble the paçocas with your hands until it's a coarse powder and place it on a large gratin dish, or place the finely chopped peanuts in the dish.

6 Melt two-thirds of the dark chocolate in a stainless steel bowl set over a saucepan of simmering water. Make sure the base of the bowl doesn't touch the water. Stir the chocolate with a spatula. As with the prior chocolate, remove the bowl from the heat before it is all melted and finish the melting by stirring it. Add the remaining dark chocolate to the bowl. Stir with a rubber spatula to melt the new chocolate into the already melted chocolate and leave it at room temperature for about 10 minutes.

7 Organise your working space with the tray of truffles on your left, the melted chocolate in the middle and the crumbled paçoca on your right. Using a chocolate fork, dip each truffle into the melted chocolate, covering the whole outside surface. Lift each truffle out of the chocolate and shake gently up and down to let the excess chocolate drop off. Immediately roll each truffle in the crumbled paçoca or chopped peanuts until it's fully covered. (Alternatively, you can sprinkle some crumbled paçoca on the top of the truffle immediately after dipping.) Let the chocolate fully set before removing them from the paçocas.

8 Store the truffles in an airtight plastic container in a dry place at a cool room temperature for up to 3 weeks.

CAIPIRINHA BONBONS

Bombom de Caipirinha

When I entertain, I like to develop new recipes and try them on my guests. For one dinner party, I thought of a creative way to present caipirinha in a sweet. Although I use a moulded bonbon technique for this recipe, you can also hand-dip them in tempered chocolate, like truffles (see Peanut Butter Truffles, page 164). If you can't find *cachaça*, this ganache is so good it's worth using another alcohol, like vodka. As a sign of a fine bonbon, the outer shell should not be too thick; but you can't make it too thin either, otherwise the shell will break. Working with good brands of chocolate is a mantra, but when it comes to making bonbons, it is pivotal. That's because a good chocolate will not only have a superb taste but also have the perfect balance between cocoa butter and cocoa solids. Too much cocoa butter makes the chocolate too thin, and too little cocoa butter, too thick. Also, different brands of chocolate behave in different ways, so once you find the one you like, stick to it. Read more about tempering chocolate on page 165.

MAKES ABOUT 50 BONBONS

450g (1lb) dark chocolate, chopped

90ml (3¼fl oz) double cream

zest of 1 lime

3 tablespoons freshly squeezed lime juice

175g (6 oz) white chocolate, chopped

1 teaspoon light corn syrup

2 tablespoons cachaça

25g (1 oz) unsalted butter, at room temperature

2 polycarbonate bonbon moulds
   (with 25 holes each)

1   Follow the instructions on page 164 to melt two-thirds of the dark chocolate for the mold. Using a ladle, divide the chocolate throughout the entire mould, filling each hole completely. Tap the sides and bottom of the mould to remove any air bubbles trapped inside. Invert the mould back over the bowl of melted chocolate, letting all the excess chocolate drip out. Tap the sides again to help remove more excess chocolate. The amount of chocolate left in each hole is critical to determine the finesse of the bonbon. Each hole should be lined with chocolate but not filled.

2   Using a chef's knife or a sharp metal spatula, scrape the top of the mould to remove the excess chocolate and turn it over so that the open holes are facing the baking paper. Allow the chocolate to set, about 5–10 minutes.

3   Turn the mould over, with the holes facing up, and leave for another 20 minutes – the chocolate has to be set and dried before filling.

4   Meanwhile, make the ganache. Place the white chocolate and corn syrup in a bowl.

5   In a small saucepan, bring the double cream and lime zest and juice to the boil over a medium heat. Immediately strain through a small sieve over the white chocolate. Leave for a few seconds, then whisk the ganache gently.

6   Make sure the ganache is room temperature before you add the butter. Add the *cachaça* and whisk.

7   Pour the ganache into a piping bag or zip-lock plastic bag. Cut a very small opening and carefully fill each hole of the mould almost to the top, leaving enough space for a thin layer of chocolate to close the moulds. Place the 2 moulds in the refrigerator and chill for 1 hour. Remove the moulds from the refrigerator 10 minutes before adding the final chocolate layer.

8   Repeat the process of tempering the remaining dark chocolate, then ladle it equally over the filled moulds, making sure each hole is full. Lightly tap the mould to remove any air bubbles.

9   Lay the 2 moulds flat on the work surface, holes facing up. Holding one tightly with one hand, scrape the mould with the other hand in one swoop to remove any excess chocolate. Don't do this more than once, or the bases of the chocolates won't be smooth. If excess chocolate drips down the sides of the mould, just clean it off with a metal spatula back into the bowl. Repeat with the other mould.

10   Let the moulds stand, holes facing up, until the chocolate sets, about 10–20 minutes. If necessary, chill the moulds in the refrigerator for a few minutes more.

11   Invert one mould, holes facing down, and gently tap against the work surface. The bonbons should easily fall out. Repeat with the second mould. Keep bonbons in an airtight plastic container at room temperature for up to 3 weeks.

BAKED COCONUT
Cocada de Forno

SERVES 6

115g (4 oz) unsalted butter, at room temperature

100g (4 oz) sugar

3 whole eggs

75ml (2½fl oz) coconut milk

100ml (3½fl oz) sweetened condensed milk

1 tablespoon Malibu

140g (5 oz) unsweetened dessicated coconut

2 tablespoons plain flour, sifted

a large baking dish

One of my favourite dishes at Brazil a Gosto, Chef Luiza Trajano's elegant restaurant in San Paulo, is a baked *cocada* (a coconut sweet made of coconut and sugar, cut into squares) with lemon sorbet. It is so delicious that I had to experiment with it back in my American kitchen. I have to admit I am very happy with the final result and I think you will be, too. This is an unpretentious and easy dessert to assemble. You can prepare everything in advance and just bake it on the day of serving.

1 Preheat the oven to 180°C/350°F/Gas Mark 4. Lightly grease a large baking dish with cooking oil.

2 In the bowl of an electric mixer fitted with the paddle attachment, mix the butter and sugar until light and creamy at medium speed, about 5 minutes. Add the eggs, one at a time, and continue to mix, scraping the side of the bowl after each addition.

3 Add the coconut milk, sweetened condensed milk and Malibu and continue to mix at medium speed until the mixture is well blended, about 1 minute. Add the coconut and mix until it is all incorporated, although the mixture will look grainy.

4 Fold the flour in with a rubber spatula. Spread the mixture into the prepared baking dish. You can keep this in the refrigerator, covered with clingfilm, up to 2 days in advance.

5 Bake in the oven until the top looks golden brown, the edges are set, but the centre is slightly nobbly, about 20 minutes. Remove it from the oven and leave to rest for 10 minutes.

6 Serve with a scoop of lemon sorbet.

GLOSSARY

Açai – Açaí
Açaí's look is similar to a blueberry in colour and size, with a seed the diameter of a pea. One berry holds very little pulp, but fortunately, the fruit grows like a weed on a type of palm tree with a slender trunk generally 25 metres high. Just about every part of the tree can be used: the fruit and its seeds, the roots, the hearts of palm and the fruit stalks. But the most esteemed harvest is the fruit itself, which produces the açai juice, extracted by a process of maceration. For cooking purposes, the fruit must be bought in its frozen pulp version, then thawed before using.

Brazil Nuts – Castanha-do-Pará
This nut comes from an enormously tall tree that can reach up to 45 metres in height, so the only way to harvest the nuts is to wait for the fruit to fall. These fruits are quite large, about the size of a melon, and each one contains between 10 and 25 nuts. The oblong nut is the part we eat and cook with, and it has a crunchy yellowish kernel with a very thin brown skin. Brazil nuts are so rich in protein that only 2 nuts are the equivalent of eating an egg. You can use the Brazil nut in a variety of recipes the way you use almonds or hazelnuts. Store them in the refrigerator or the freezer inside a ziplock bag.

Brazilian Cream Cheese – Requeijão
Brazilians are absolutely crazy for this mild flavoured cream cheese. Like so many of our culinary treasures, it started back in colonial times when slaves were given sour milk. By leaving the milk to sit, the fat in the milk separates, but it's then incorporated back into the curd by slowly mixing the two together over a low heat. Depending on the consistency of the requeijão, a little or a lot of milk is also added. In Brazil, one of my favourite brands of requeijão is Catupiry, available in many Brazilian stores. It's the brand I use for the recipes in this book.

Cachaça
Cachaça is a distilled beverage from Brazil, as important to the country as vodka is to Russia and tequila is to Mexico. Essentially it is an aguardente – a spirit distilled from fruits or vegetables – in this case, the juices of the sugarcane. Cachaça is distinct from rum though, which is made from the molasses not the cane's juice. The spirit was invented in the mid-1500s in Brazil, when Portuguese colonisers began to cultivate sugarcane. Somewhere in a sugar mill around São Paulo, some stems of rough sugarcane were forgotten and yielded a foamy, nonalcoholic juice that naturally fermented. The drink had a strong effect on the body, was frequently used as a painkiller, and it was served to slaves for centuries. Eventually the Portuguese decided to distill and age it, creating a new type of aguardente and named it cachaça. There are many different kinds of wood (oak, cherry, and jequitibá rosa among them) used for ageing the spirit, each leaving different traces of taste – some with a more floral flavour, others with a hint of vanilla or cinnamon.

Chayote – Chuchu or Xuxu
Chayote is a tender squash from the same family as melons, cucumbers and squash. When handling chayote, the vegetable releases oil that sticks to our hands like wax – which is why often you'll see them individually wrapped in plastic. I simply wear gloves when handling it while other Brazilians peel it under running water.

Coconut milk – Leite de Côco
Despite the name, coconut milk contains no dairy whatsoever; the "milk" is nothing but coconut blended with hot water, then strained. Although it is quite easy to make at home, coconut milk can be found in any supermarket and has become a common storecupboard ingredient in many a home kitchen. Most coconut milks are sold tinned or in a glass bottle and they can sit for a long time in your storecupboard (while the homemade version will last only a few days in the refrigerator). Make sure you shake the can or bottle well before using it. Sometimes, the coconut milk can solidify so much that shaking is not enough. In this case, place the unopened tin or bottle in a bowl with hot water for 20 minutes to help liquefy it again. If your coconut milk is too thick, you can always thin it out with a few teaspoons of warm water.

Different brands of coconut milk might present a small variation in sweetness and consistency. I use a Brazilian brand, Sococo, for all my recipes because I find it has the purest taste of coconut, with less sweetness, and the best consistency of all coconut milks. Other brands such as Goya or Thai are good, too.

Cupuaçu – Cupuaçú
Cupuaçu is a fruit that grows in the Amazon in the same family as the cacao. The pulp, which is separated from the seeds, has a very strong and alcoholic taste. Due to its high acidity, it's never consumed raw, but freezes quite well. Cupuaçu is used in Brazil in hundreds of different recipes, from mousses, ice creams, puddings, pies and cakes. Most likely cupuaçu won't reach the supermarket in its true form anytime soon, but you will find cupuaçu being sold in a pasteurised and frozen form. Make the mistake of trying to eat it thawed and you'll never go near it again. Cook with the pulp, and you will, like me, fall in love with it (see my recipe on page 156). I like to buy it directly from www.kajafruit.com, or whenever I see it in the freezer of a specialist shop.

Dendê oil – Azeite de Dendê
This oil is the mainstay of Bahian cuisine, and is the product extracted from the dendê palm tree, which was brought to Brazil by African slaves, back in the seventeenth century. The dendê palm tree is one of the most oleaginous in the world, producing more oil then soya beans, peanuts or coconut. The fruit and the pit are used in two different ways. The dendê oil used in cooking is extracted from the fruit pulp; first it is cooked in steam, then it is dried completely in the sun. The fruit is then crushed to release its bright orange-red oil. The pit is also used to extract oil of a different kind, with a transparent colour, mostly used for cosmetics for its similarity to cocoa butter. Often sediment forms on the bottom of a dendê oil bottle. To liquefy, simply place the bottle in a bowl with warm water and let it sit for 20 minutes.

Dulce de leche – Doce de Leite
This is truly a Latin ingredient produced and used all over South America. In Brazil, the state of Minas Gerais is the heart of Brazil's dairy country and the biggest producer of the best dulche de leche. Essentially, dulche de leche is milk and sugar cooked slowly until it reaches the consistency of a caramelised paste. In Brazil we eat dolche de leche in all kinds of consistencies: as a candy, as a soft paste,

hard paste, more sweet, less sweet, even diet. For all of the recipes in this book, I used tinned Nestlé dulce de leche.

Jerk Meat – Carne Seca

Jerk meat or dried meat is a huge part of Brazilian cooking. In Portuguese we also call it *carne de sol*, referring to salt-cured and sun-dried meat. Most jerk meats come from a lean cut, such as the flank, because too much marbled fat (what gives that buttery richness we want in our cooked meats) makes the dried meat too tough. Most pieces of jerk meat are cut against the grain to make them tender rather than leathery. In other cuisines, the processes of making jerk beef vary greatly, from salting to brining, smoking in hickory or oak, or not smoking at all. Flavouring can be introduced with a dry rub, a paste or a marinade. Drying can take place in commercial ovens, dehydrators or naturally. The Brazilian method is less elaborate. While many of the ingredients found in this country are comparable to those found in Brazil, jerk meat is the exception so it might taste a little different from the one eaten in Brazil. Most specialist Brazilian shops carry a ready-made version of prepared *carne seca* that I use in some of the recipes in this book.

Linguiça

Linguiça is a type of sausage typical from Portugal and brought to Brazil during colonial times. Today linguiça is the most adored sausage in Brazil, served in *churrascarias* (our barbecue restaurants), as hors d'oeuvres and in dishes such as *feijoada, farofa,* soups and braises. The robust sausage is made from cured pork meat and flavored with onion, garlic and condiments. When cooking linguiça, never poke the link, you don't want any fat to escape, as this is what makes the linguiça taste so moist and tender in the centre. If you can't find it, you can use chorizo or fresh sausage as well.

Manioc Starch

Manioc starch *(povilho doce)* and sour manioc starch *(povilho azedo)* are both extracted from yucca. The vegetable is first grated, then washed and its pulp is squeezed over a bucket. The starch accumulated in the bucket is then extracted from the liquid, which is then dried and sifted. The difference between them is a natural fermentation process undergone by the sour starch when it is left at room temperature for a period of 15 days to ferment. The manioc starch has a much finer consistency and more delicate texture than the sour manioc starch and is mostly used in sweets and crackers.

Although it may sound a little confusing, don't mistake manioc starch for manioc flour. It gets even more confusing because in English, manioc starch is usually called tapioca flour. So here are a few useful terms with quick translations:

Farinha de mandioca = manioc flour (used to make *farofa*)

Povilho doce = manioc starch = tapioca flour (used to make *pao de queijo* and other baked goods)

Povilho azedo = fermented, sour manioc starch = fermented tapioca flour, found in any Brazilian store (also used to make pao de queijo and other baking goods). Yoke is a brand widely available in the United States and Europe.

Minas Cheese

Minas cheese is to Brazil what feta is to Greece, or what mozzarella is to Italy. The taste is also a cross between a feta, a ricotta and mozzarella. Brazilians eat Minas cheese throughout the country, but Mineiros (people born in Minas Gerais) are really proud to have created it in their state of Minas Gerais, hence the name. Minas cheese, made from cow's milk, is white, fresh and firm. Like other fresh white cheeses, Minas has a way of complementing other flavours without masking them, and it definitely deserves more attention on its own. It is mostly consumed fresh but the cheese can also be ripened to various degrees: *fresco* (fresh), *meia-cura* (semi-ripened) and *curado* (ripened).

Plantain – Banana-da Terra

The plantain is a first cousin of the common banana. Unlike its cousin though, it cannot be eaten raw. It is larger and starchier than a banana and very versatile: It can be mashed, fried, baked or braised. It's easy to find plantains year-round at most supermarkets, especially Latin and Asian specialty stores. You can always buy them online at retailers like Melissa's (www.melissas.com). Plantains can be used at every stage of ripeness for diverse results. When the peel is green, the flesh is very firm and starchy, almost like a potato. When the peel is semiripe, it looks yellow with lots of black specks, and the fruit is sweeter and still starchy. When the peel is black and shrivelled, the fruit is softer, less starchy and at its sweetest.

Salt Cod – Bacalhau Salgado

Salt cod arrived on the Brazilian table through our colonisers, and today Brazil is the biggest consumer of salt cod followed by Portugal, Spain and Italy. Brazil however, is not a producer – all our product is imported from Norway and Portugal. Brazilians rarely eat fresh cod as it's just not available to us. The Vikings were the first to learn the process of preserving fish by hanging it in the air, causing the fish to lose weight and become a hard plank – perfectly suited for transportation and trade. Once reconstituted, it presents a flaky flesh that is absolutely delicious. The best species of cod for salting is the Atlantic cod, *Gadus morhua*. When using salt cod, it's very important to desalt it properly: Use a big plastic container as the volume of water has to be at least 10 times bigger than the weight of the cod. I also like to use a rack or colander so the cod is floating completely in the water. Try to find cod that has thick flesh.

Yucca

This tuber vegetable also goes by the names manioc or cassava. Earthier tasting than a potato and richer in starch, this vegetable is one of the foundations of Brazilian cooking. It comes from a perennial shrub with origins in the Amazon. The plant's long roots grow in clusters and are covered in a thick, shiny brown skin and a thick white layer. When cut off, the outer layers reveal a snow white, firm interior with grey or purple veins. The centre of the vegetable also carries a woody fibre that is not pleasant to eat, but is easy to remove. Riper yuccas usually contain less fibre in their centres. Generally speaking, the thicker the yucca, the riper it is. There are so many derivatives of this one vegetable: toasted flour, flakes, starches, juices. Even the skin and leaves are used in some parts of Brazil. For home use, yucca is mostly boiled or fried and becomes very creamy with a mellow taste. When buying yucca, try to look for an even coloured vegetable with slightly waxy brown skin and no soft or mouldy spots. Many of the yuccas sold in the United States are coated with a thin layer of wax to help extend its shelf life.

INDEX

ACKNOWLEDGEMENTS

If it wasn't for the encouragement of some very special and talented people, this project wouldn't have happened. It all started when my husband Dean Schwartz introduced to me Charlie Wing, an incredible author, who is a great inspiration. He led me to Dolores York, who saw this project grow from a teeny-weeny-seed into a book. Thank you both, so much! Thanks to Jane Stern, who encouraged me to walk with my own legs, and gave me great insights all along the way.

Thanks to Alan Richman and David Leite for making me exercise the skill of writing, always coaching me with supreme technique, and helping me find a manner of therapy in writing.

Thanks to my incredible agent Joy Tutela, for helping me shape my ideas, guiding me with decency and professionalism, and for always being stable and strong during this wild ride and its many sharp turns. And to everyone at David Black Literary Agency who helped with this project, in particular, many thanks to Luke Thomas, who helped with the manuscript.

At Kyle Books, thanks to Kyle Cathie for welcoming this project into her house and to my editor, Anja Schmidt, for embracing my ideas and shaping them into this book – always with a warm and collaborative spirit.

Thanks to amazing photographers Luciano Bogado, who took many of the market shots in Brazil, and to Ben Fink, who photographed all the finished dishes. Thank you both for making this book such a visual joy.

Thanks to Roy Finamore for his creative prop styling, and his expertise on the industry was a great contribution. Thanks to Susan Varanajan for styling the food so beautifully for the camara. Jee Chang captured the spirit and colours of Brazil into the design of this book – thanks for your beautiful work.

Thanks to recipe testers: Martha Schueneman, Cynthia Kruth, Alicia Kirchhof, Nicole Carpino, and Richard Schulman. Thanks to Chef Georges Mendes for letting me peek into his kitchen at Aldea and sharing the best *Arroz de Pato* I've ever eaten.

Obrigado ao meu maravilhoso analista José Alberto Zusman, que me ajudou a descobrir a minha verdadeira paixão pela culinaria – sua voz está sempre comigo, mesmo a muitos kilometros de distância.

Obrigado ao meu irmão e amigo Jimmy Benzaquen, a quem eu confio e consulto como uma fonte de sabedoria, sua esposa Fernanda e minha sobrinha Valentina por abençoar nossas familias com alegria.

Obrigado a meus pais Selma e Salomon Benzaquen, que sempre me fizeram sentir amada e me apoiaram a mudar de carreira e buscar o meu sonho em outro país. Voces são os pais mais normais, estáveis, e sábios que eu conheco, e a fonte de inspiração para o jeito que eu amo os meus próprios filhos.

My husband, my best friend, my biggest supporter – Dean, who brings his laptop to the kitchen to stay with me while I am cooking the fifth version of *Toucinho do Céu* late at night – thanks for understanding my obsession, for embarking on this journey with me and for your infinite love. To my children Thomas and Bianca – who are the greatest joy and the balance in my life.

I cherish my friendship with Dina Cheney, Patty Pulliam and Arnaldo Dines – thanks for everything. It would be hard to list all of my Brazilian and American friends, with whom I have shared so many meals. Thanks for all the good times we shared together enjoying health, children, life, and so many recipes in this book. Thanks to the Riback family for your love and support since day one.

Obrigado aos feirantes de Ipanema no Rio de Janeiro pelas frutas maravilhosas.

E obrigado ao meu país – Brasil, que me fez e me faz tão feliz. E um privilégio e alegria poder representar a nossa cozinha e nossa cultura nesse livro.